Swift, Silent and Deadly:
Recon Marine Heroes in Vietnam

Michael J. Schneider

DEDICATION

This book is dedicated to all the Marines who served in reconnaissance units in Vietnam, their families, and friends. I owe a debt of gratitude to those Recon Marines who survived their time in Vietnam and were willing to share their stories. I'm also indebted to those family members who provided in depth information to more fully characterize some of the Marines included in this book.

Swift, Silent and Deadly:
Recon Marine Heroes in Vietnam

Table of Contents

ILLUSTRATIONS

Introduction

When I was a senior in high school in 1968, the Vietnam War was at its height. The United States had approximately 500,000 troops serving in the Vietnam War at that time, and the need for manpower in Vietnam was so great that the government was offering to pay the cost of four years of college tuition for anyone who served a minimum of two years in active duty. As a high school graduate with no resources to attend college, and likely to be drafted before turning nineteen, I decided to take advantage of this opportunity. Serving one's county during wartime was familiar to me since my father had served in the Navy during World War II and the Korean War, and my mother in the Marine Corps during World War II.

I viewed with interest the television news programs which featured Marines in action during the Vietnam conflict. In particular, I was impressed by reports on the siege of Khe Sanh in early 1968 where 6,000 Marine and Army troops were surrounded by 20,000 to 30,000 Communist troops bent on seizing this remote outpost. The Marine commander vowed to hold on and the American troops were victorious. For me it was reminiscent of the Alamo, except our troops were not defeated. This type of action influenced my decision to enlist in the Marine Corps.

After boot camp and four additional weeks of infantry training, I was sent to a four week school to be trained for an administrative position. After a twenty day leave, I reported to Staging Battalion at Camp Pendleton, California. Here all Marines underwent three more weeks of training to prepare them for Vietnam. I was pulled from my staging unit on the first day and assigned the duty of processing other Marines going through Staging Battalion. After approximately two months, I requested transfer because I would not be promoted while working in Staging Battalion. I was then assigned to a unit that had already completed their staging training and was ready to depart for Vietnam.

I arrived in Da Nang, Republic of Vietnam, on October 3, 1969. While most of the other Marines with whom I arrived were assigned to units at the casual barracks in Da Nang, I was sent to 1st Marine Division Headquarters for assignment. From there I was assigned to Headquarters and Service Company (H&S Company,) 1st Reconnaissance Battalion at Camp Reasoner. As you will read in this book, Camp Reasoner was named after a Marine Medal of Honor recipient.

I worked at H&S Company from October 1969 through April 1970. I had never formally learned to type, so I spent more hours at administrative work than the other clerks assigned to H&S Company. In addition, I spent four or five nights a week on night duty in the office or on guard duty in a bunker on the ridgeline which was part of the 1st Marine Division defense perimeter. During this time, I thought I could better serve the Marine Corps as an infantryman. I made several requests for transfer to my Company commander, Captain Wiltrout. He tried to convince me that I would still be assigned as a clerk with an infantry unit and that living conditions at Camp Reasoner were far superior to those I would encounter in the "bush". As a concession, however, he arranged with his favorite handball partner, Captain McVey, the commander of Charlie Company, to send me with a platoon of Reconnaissance Marines assigned to man an observation post in the "bush". I enjoyed being on the observation post. We would work half of a day building up perimeter defenses. I had to pull a few hours of guard duty each night, but the rest of the time we were able to relax, mostly reading books. It was a vacation compared to my duties at H&S Company. Recon platoons normally spent two weeks on observation posts after which they were relieved by another platoon. However, I was pulled off after only one week because my 1st Sergeant wanted me back in the office to help prepare for a big administrative inspection. Later, the 1st Sergeant promised me that after the inspection he would try to have me assigned to a reconnaissance company. He kept his promise and on May 11, 1970 I began training with newly arrived Reconnaissance Marines in a program called Reconnaissance Indoctrination Program (RIP).

Upon completion of the RIP program I was assigned to a reconnaissance team with Bravo Company. At that time the company commander was 1st Lieutenant Dennis Storm. The platoon to which I was assigned was ordered to man an observation post on Hill 250. We stayed there for two weeks. The only event of note which I recall was a visit from the commanding general of the 1st Marine Division. I was not able to meet him as I was on duty guarding the landing zone (LZ) while his helicopter was on the ground. Later, however, I did enjoy some of the ice cream which the general brought to the observation post (OP.)

After returning from the OP, I participated in four long range reconnaissance patrols. On two of these patrols we had a short contact with the enemy. On the first patrol, our point man spotted two enemy soldiers at the crest of a trail. When the point man ordered them to surrender, one of the enemy soldiers tried to fire at him. The point man fired first and hit the enemy who then dropped his AK-47 rifle and disappeared into the brush, along with the other enemy soldier. Our team picked up the AK-47 and a discarded pack. Shortly after, a helicopter arrived to extract us as our position would now be known to the enemy.

On the last of my four patrols, our point man also encountered two enemy soldiers doing laundry in a stream. He fired at them but they disappeared into the brush. We were ordered to leave the immediate area and call an artillery strike on the position where the enemy had been spotted. When the artillery strike was over, we were ordered to resume the patrol. There no further encounters over the next four days.

I was preparing for my fifth patrol when I was told to report to the company office. The 1st Sergeant told me I was to report to Charlie Company to serve in an administrative position again. I was quite disappointed. On the fifth patrol I would have been the primary radioman. The 1st Sergeant and Lieutenant Storm explained that a directive had come down from Division Headquarters that no more administrative personnel would be assigned to the Battalion, but rather, they were to remain in their specialty. As Lieutenant Storm put it, "When the Battalion Commander calls me Dennis, I'm free to argue with him, but when he addresses me as Lieutenant, I have to shut up and obey his orders. Likewise when I call you Mike you can argue with me, but when I call you Lance Corporal there is nothing more to discuss."

My very short career as a Reconnaissance Marine was over. I spent the next two months as a clerk with Charlie Company. I extended my Vietnam tour three months so I could take a second R&R (a vacation) to Australia.

Afterwards, I was assigned back to Bravo Company because Charlie Company had shipped out of Vietnam. I was forced to remain a clerk with Bravo Company for the rest of my tour in Vietnam which ended December 13, 1970.

In November 1970, the tragedy I describe in this book involving *Rush Act* occurred. The Navy Corpsman on that team, Doc Daniels, shared living quarters with me prior to his death. He was a great guy and you will get to read more about him later.

This book contains several stories of Reconnaissance Marines in Vietnam. I wrote this book because I felt that while there are many books available on the Vietnam War, not enough are written with the young adult reader in mind. It is my hope that these stories of war heroes will serve to inspire and make an impression on this young teenage audience.

Chapter 1 - Recons Role in the War

Imagine being one of a six-man team in the middle of a jungle where any person you might encounter might try to kill you. This is hostile territory, inhabited by an unknown number of enemy soldiers, so you could encounter 1 or 2 of them, or just as easily 50 or more. There is also the danger of man-eating tigers and poisonous snakes lurking in the jungle. Your mission is to find the enemy without them finding you. You are to report their position so that artillery batteries, bombers or helicopter gunships can destroy the enemy without risking the lives of infantrymen in a hazardous jungle assault. You must keep quiet or you will be heard. The brush is so thick it's hard not snap twigs or crunch brush as you move. You find a trail; but you can't walk on it because it may be booby-trapped with land mines. What sort of men are willing to undertake such a mission?

These men are Reconnaissance Marines (Recon Marines for short). In the conflict between the United States and

Vietnam they played a vital role in locating and destroying the enemy. To understand why they were so special, you must know something of the Vietnam War and the environment in which it was fought.

The War: Vietnam was a French colony prior to World War II. In 1940, the Japanese wrested control of the country from the French. A man named Ho Chi Minh organized an army of rebels called the Vietminh to resist the Japanese. When the Vietminh finally ousted the Japanese during World War II, the French sought to rule Vietnam as a colony again. When the French returned, the Vietminh turned their efforts to try to drive them out also.

In 1954, the Communist Vietminh finally won over the French. At that time, so many countries had fallen under the totalitarianism of Communist rule, the free countries, the United States included, opposed any further expansion of Communism. In addition, communists didn't believe in God and sought to repress the practice of religion. Since many Vietnamese were Catholics, those people resisted being dominated by the communist Vietminh. For these reasons, the country became divided into North and South Vietnam with the communists under Ho Chi Minh controlling the North and an anti-communist regime under Ngo Dinh Diem in the South.

This division into two Vietnam's was supposed to be a temporary situation with both sides agreeing to elections to be held at a future date to elect leaders who would reunify the two countries.

The elections never took place. Instead, the communists became more aggressive and a group called the National Liberation Front (more commonly called the Viet Cong) formed in the south. The Viet Cong terrorized the rest of the population through murder and torture in an effort to gain control of the south.

Not wanting South Vietnam to fall to the communists,

the United States decided to support the anti-communist forces in their fight against the Viet Cong and the North Vietnamese Army. At first we only sent advisors to help train the South Vietnamese army. By 1965, however, the Army of the Republic of Vietnam (ARVN) was still too weak to resist the extremely aggressive communist forces. The United States Government decided it would take a major commitment of combat troops to help liberate South Vietnam from the scourge of the communists. In March of 1965 the first Marines arrived in Vietnam.

By 1969, the number of Marines in Vietnam reached its maximum. The Marine commander of the III Marine Amphibious Force was responsible for the defense of the Republic of Vietnam's (South Vietnam) five northernmost provinces. This included the 1st and 3rd Marine Divisions, the 1st Marine Aircraft Wing, numerous other smaller Marine combat and support units, and some U.S. Army Units. This area was known as I Corps Tactical Zone, usually just called I Corps. Reconnaissance units provided the information the Marine generals needed to plan successful combat operations against the communist forces in these provinces of I Corps.

The Enemy: The enemy the Marines faced was composed of two main groups. The first was the Viet Cong, also known as the VC. These were fighters that were not regular soldiers. They often lived among the other people in villages and cities of Vietnam. They would gather together at night or in remote areas to prepare for an attack on American or ARVN forces. The VC were predominately South Vietnamese communists.

The second group was the North Vietnamese Army or NVA. These were regular army troops from North Vietnam, sent south to assist the Viet Cong in taking control of South Vietnam. They would "infiltrate" South Vietnam. That is, when the NVA came down from the north, they would stick to the jungle or remote areas where their movement would not likely be noticed.

Both the VC and NVA engaged primarily in guerrilla warfare. This means they usually would strike a target, for example, a village or a city, then retreat back into the jungle or blend in with the rest of the population where they wouldn't be noticed. The Americans, generally used to fighting battles on a large scale, had a difficult time fighting this elusive enemy.

Weapons and Tactics: U.S. Marines are generally assault forces. Traditionally they traveled aboard navy ships where they could be sent ashore to deal with trouble Americans might have with foreign nations. During World War II, they fought almost exclusively in the Pacific Theater of the war. In this war they perfected the technique of the amphibious landing, which is, landing on the beach from the sea and moving inland to defeat the enemy and take control of an island. Vietnam, however, provided a different challenge. While the Marines made some amphibious landings, they didn't engage the enemy on the beach. In fact, when the Marines first landed in northern South Vietnam in 1965 their mission was primarily to defend critical areas (airfields for instance) against attack by the VC or NVA. As more Marines arrived in South Vietnam, they took on a more offensive role. The northern part of South Vietnam contains a lot of jungle-covered mountains. The Marines soon learned that the most efficient way to transport troops from a base camp to an area where the enemy had been spotted was by helicopter. Although a variety of helicopters were used, those used most often were cargo helicopters and gunships. Cargo helicopters ferried both troops and supplies from one place to another.

An example is the CH-46, which has a large tube-shaped body with rotors on both the front and rear. Near the front, machine guns are mounted on both sides where machine gunners on the crew can provide covering fire if the troops being transported needed to be rescued from a battle in the field.

CH-46 Helicopter

The gunship is a helicopter specially designed to attack the enemy. An example is the Cobra. It carries a crew of two and delivers a stream of bullets from its machine guns or grenades from its grenade launcher. The gunships usually accompanied the cargo helicopters when the trip involved entering an area where the cargo helicopters might draw enemy fire.

Artillery played an important role also. The big guns were placed at various locations within the Marines area of responsibility where they could support troops engaged with the enemy in the field. These locations were called Fire Support Bases.

Air support was available also. Jets from an aircraft carrier or from an air base in South Vietnam flew missions in support of the ground forces, often delivering bombs or napalm, a chemical, which can spread and burn a large area. At times long-range bombers would fly missions to South Vietnam

Cobra Helicopter Gunship

from Okinawa and deliver heavy bombardment known as "Arc Light".

Since the "hit and run" tactics used by the communist forces rarely resulted in major battles, the Marines usually had to look for the enemy. Infantry units would sweep through an area trying to find enemy soldiers and destroy any weapons or supplies the enemy might have stashed away. In order to make these operations more successful, Marine leaders used a specially trained group of Marines called Reconnaissance Marines.

Mission of the Recon Marine: The main mission of the reconnaissance Marines was to locate the enemy and their base camps. Within the jungles of Vietnam, the VC and NVA had developed an intricate system of trails and supply points to keep themselves supplied with weapons, ammunition, food and other items need to conduct war. Reconnaissance Marines searched for these places where enemy forces might be concentrated, and reported their locations back to headquarters where the decision would be made whether to attack with infantry troops, artillery, air strikes or some combination of the three.

Often the Recon Marines, who were to be "Swift, Silent & Deadly", would run into or be discovered by the enemy. Such an encounter was called "making contact". The Marines would then have to fight off the enemy while trying to escape being overwhelmed.
Sometimes Recon Marines would conduct raids themselves; but this was not their primary mission. More commonly, they would call in artillery or air strikes on the targets when they discovered them in the bush.

Training: Recon Marines started with the same basic training as other U.S. Marines. As a result of basic training, all Marines become proficient in the use of their primary weapon, the rifle. It is often quoted; "The deadliest animal on the earth is a Marine Rifleman." Most commonly, this rifle was the M-14 or M-16. The M-16 replaced the M-14 as the weapon generally issued during the later years of the war

Recon Marines, however received training unique to their task. First, of course, is physical training. In the field a Recon Marine would have to carry heavy packs and other personal gear over rough terrain in unbearable heat. Running

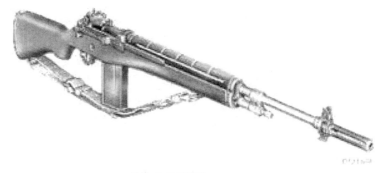

M-14 Rifle

M-16 Rifle

3 miles or more on a daily basis was the core of the Recon Marine's training.

Information was the main product of a reconnaissance mission. For this reason a lot of training focused on the gathering and communicating of information. Instructors taught classes on reporting procedures, what to look for in the handling of captured documents and equipment, how to communicate over the radio, how to care for the radio, how to care for and use cameras.

Typically a reconnaissance patrol was composed of 7 men. One of these was a Navy Corpsman who was specially trained in emergency medical procedures to assist a wounded or injured Marine. However, in the event something happened to the Corpsman, each Marine had to know some basic first aid. A Recon Marine's training included this.

The Recon Marine also had to be trained in what to look for in the handling of captured documents and equipment. Often important information could be deduced about the enemy from the things the enemy was carrying. Another important skill was map reading. If you didn't know where you were, it would be virtually impossible for the helicopters to find you and pull you out of the bush. Skill in map reading also had other important consequences. One could avoid being trapped on a cliff or otherwise forced into some terrain where the enemy had the advantage. In addition, knowing where one was allowed you to call the artillery battery and they could shoot rounds to help fight off the enemy.

One of the actual fun parts of the training was rappelling. This involved jumping from a high place to the ground while using a rope to keep from falling too fast. Two types of rappelling were important. The first was rappelling from a cliff. To practice this a Recon Marine would jump off a 30-foot tower. The other kind was rappelling from a helicopter. In a way, this was much easier. The reason is that you didn't have to worry about hitting anything on the way down. Marines typically learned rappelling from a CH-46 Sea Knight helicopter. It had a square hole in the bottom of the fuselage known as the "Hell hole" The CH-46 also had a back ramp, from which Marines could also rappel. Rappelling was a quick way to get a recon team to the ground when the helicopter could not find a suitable place to land.

Another fun part of the training was the rubber boat drills. Since it was not uncommon that recon marines might be launched on a mission from submarines, the marines had to know how to handle a rubber boat. In the rubber boats, the Marines learned how to paddle in a coordinated manner and how to deal with the boat capsizing. When the boat capsized, the Marines learned how to empty the water from it and set it upright again. These were called broaching drills. As you might guess, being able to swim is a valuable and necessary skill for a Recon Marine.

Tactics: Since a Marine recon team was not an offensive unit, the tactics they learned were mainly those needed to avoid detection and how to react when encountering the enemy. Some of the things the Marines would do to avoid detection included staying off traveled trails, avoiding talking out loud, and burying or packing out any trash from their rations.

The Reconnaissance Marine also trained in patrolling techniques. One of the skills he had to learn was how to React when a patrol made contact with the enemy. A Recon

New recon member learns to repel.

Techniques of rubber boat landing are learned.

Marine could expect to practice immediate action (IA) drills. In IA drills each member of the team practices what moves to make if the team encounters the enemy. Normally the team forms a circle, which they called a "360" after the number of degrees in a circle. The Marine closest to the enemy would fire a magazine of ammunition at the enemy, then run through the circle, stop and reload. The Marine second closest to the enemy would then fire a magazine and follow the first. The remaining team members followed in turn. By the time all had done so, they would have formed a new 360, ready to repeat if necessary. At this time the team leader would order what action to take next. A recon team would practice these drills over and over until they became a reflexive reaction. The drills included what to do if being attacked from the front, rear, or the flanks.

Immediate Action (IA) Drills

Since it is important for a Recon Marine to work and rely on an artillery battery, he also received training on being a forward observer. A forward observer is one spots an enemy target and tells the men firing the big guns how to hit the target. Normally the artillery unit may be miles away from the target and can't see it. The forward observer gives position (map coordinates) to the battery as well as the position of the enemy target. One of the big guns will fire a round at the target. The forward observer then tells the battery where the round landed and recommends a correction to aiming the big guns. This way the artillery battery can "zero in" on the target until they hit it. To learn how to do this, the Recon Marine receives training on the capabilities of the artillery guns. Then he practices by calling in rounds on a practice target.

To complete training, the Recon Marine goes on a practice patrol to put all his training to use. In Vietnam, there was a special place where newly arrived Recon Marines from the United States could practice their patrolling techniques. This place was Monkey Mountain. Here the vegetation was so dense and difficult to move through, that it might take half a day for a team to move 1000 yards.

Weapons: A Recon Marine learned to use a variety of weapons. Nearest and dearest to his heart was his rifle. All Marines are first and foremost riflemen. Recon Marines were certainly no exception. The M-14 and M-16 rifles were the weapons carried by the individual team members. Generally the M-16 replaced the M-14 as the standard rifle in Vietnam because of its lighter weight. The M-16 fired a 5.52 mm bullet. It could be fired semi-automatic or fully automatic. The M-14, on the other hand, normally was fired only as a semi-automatic weapon. It could, however, be converted to an automatic weapon. The M-14 fired a 7.62 mm bullet. This heavier bullet was more likely to stop VC or NVA soldier in his path immediately, so some Marines, particularly those who had to walk "point" or the lead position on a patrol, preferred to carry the M-14. The M-14 was also easier to take apart and clean if it got dirty or a round stuck in the chamber.

All the Marines on a team carried grenades. Most of these were HE or high explosive grenades. They were round in shape, and had a short delay before exploding. When thrown at the enemy, the subsequent explosion would hurl bits of metal (called shrapnel) at the enemy soldiers.

Claymore mines were another weapon carried by a recon team. These consisted of a bunch of little projectiles (they looked like the bb's used in a bb-gun) backed by C-4 plastic explosive. Normally, the team set out the mines to protect their position or "Harbor Site" at night. In the morning they would retrieve the mines again. In the event of an enemy attack, the mines would explode when a Marine closed a remote switch.

Claymore Mine

High Explosive (HE) Hand Grenade

Usually one member of a recon team also carried an M-79 grenade launcher. This weapon, commonly called "The Blooper," fired bullet-shaped grenades, 40 mm in diameter. It got its pet name from the sound it made when it was fired. It looked like a sawed-off shotgun of large diameter.

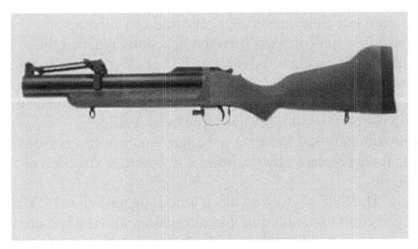

M-79 Grenade Launcher

Marines were also trained to use the M-60 machine gun, although it wasn't normally carried on patrol. This was commonly used as a defensive weapon on observation posts (OP's), which the Recon Marines guarded.

Other Special Equipment: In addition to the weapons, Recon Marines were trained to use other special equipment. One of these was C-4 plastic explosive. A common use of this explosive was to clear trees or shrubs from an LZ (Landing Zone). It was a white substance, moldable as clay and thus very practical.

The Starlight scope was another useful tool. While not normally carried on patrol, it would more likely be used when a recon team was assigned to a listening post near an OP or some other defensive perimeter. This scope allowed the viewer to see thing at night that would not normally be visible. Although the screen appeared in in a monochrome of green and yellowish-white, one could clearly distinguish individual objects, for example snakes, in the dark.

To remove a team from the bush when a helicopter landing wasn't possible, two methods were used. The first of these was the extract ladder. This was a flexible ladder, composed of aluminum rungs. It could be rolled up and carried on a helicopter. When the helicopter reached the location of the team to be extracted, the ladder was unfurled from the helicopter and the team climbed aboard it. Once all the team was on the helicopter would take off with the team dangling on the ladder below. The extract ladder, approximately 100 feet long unfurled, was still cumbersome to use. It was replaced by the Special Insertion/Extraction or SPIE rig.

The SPIE rig looked like a long rope with metal "D" shaped rings embedded in it at intervals of about 8 feet apart. There were enough of these links that each member of a complete recon team could attach themselves to the rig. For this purpose each member of the team wore a special harness that also had a snap link shaped like a "D" which could quickly be linked to one of the links on the SPIE rig. To perform an extraction, the crew on the helicopter only had to lower the rig under the helicopter low enough so the team on the ground could link on to it. The helicopter would then climb to a suitable altitude with the team dangling below. When arriving back at base, the helicopter would slowly descend, allowing the team members to touch the ground and unhook themselves from the rig.

Of course the recon team depended on the radio. Most commonly, this was the PRC-25. The team carried two of these. If one failed, the other served as a backup. They were carried as a backpack. The primary radioman carried one. Another member of the team carried the other one. The primary radio operator carried codes (called "shackle sheets"). Any information that could be useful to the enemy he translated into code before sending it. All members of the

PRC-25 Radio

Marines on SPIE Rig

team could operate the radio in an emergency; but the primary operator had received special training and was more proficient at the job.

    The Team: During the course of the Vietnam War, the Marine Corps varied the number and composition of members on the team. The most common, however, was the 7-man team composed of a point man, patrol leader, radio operator, Corpsman, secondary radioman, assistant patrol leader, and tail man. These positions are listed in the normal order of march. The team walked single file, with each member staying about 25 yards apart from the person in front and the person in back of him. This was necessary to minimize the damage enemy land mines or "booby traps" might cause if a team member accidentally set one off. The distance would reduce the likelihood that a second team member would be seriously injured or killed. Nevertheless, each team member, kept the man in front of and behind him in view. This was important because a team member would not want to get separated from the rest of the team. In addition, team members communicated with each other with hand signals so they would not give away their position by talking.

An officer or a noncommissioned officer served as a team leader. The team leader typically had a lot of experience from past patrols. The point man always went first. The team leader didn't walk point, because the point man would be the one most likely to encounter the enemy first and had the greatest risk of being shot. It was important that the team leader be able to direct the team if contact was made with the enemy. The team leader walked in the second position. This put him in view of the point position and close to his primary radioman. The functions of the Corpsman and primary radioman were discussed above. The assistant team leader and secondary radioman served as back-ups to the primary positions and as additional riflemen if the team encountered trouble. The most important function performed by the man in the rear was to look for signs of being followed. A really good rear guard could almost walk backwards the whole patrol.

Chapter 2 - Frank Reasoner (1st Marine Medal of Honor Winner)

Camp Reasoner, located about 3 miles north of Danang, Republic of Vietnam, was the base camp for many of the reconnaissance Marines who served in Vietnam. At Camp Reasoner the Marines enjoyed many of the comforts associated with being stationed in the United States: hot food, cots to sleep on, buildings called hootches with corrugated metal roofs to shed the rain and screens to keep out the mosquitoes. Other amenities available to the Marines at Camp Reasoner included an outdoor amphitheater, a handball court, a laundry, and two clubs, one for the enlisted men, the other for Staff Non-commissioned Officers, and Commissioned Officers. The clubs mainly served beverages, beer for instance, and varieties of soft drinks. The purpose of this chapter is not to talk about the camp; but the man who gave it his name.

Frank Reasoner came from Kellogg, Idaho. He was a very ambitious youngster. At the age of nine he started earning his own way with a paper route. In spite of only growing to 5 ft 7 inches tall, he played football, baseball, and basketball in high school. Frank liked boxing the best. To excel at this sport, worked out with weights and trained incessantly. By the time he graduated from high school, he had a new ambition, The United States Marine Corps.

After enlisting at the age of seventeen and completing boot camp, Frank sought a new goal, to be an officer. Without a college education, however, it wasn't possible to get those lieutenant's bars. College cost money and enlisted Marines didn't make that much, so Frank decided to try for an appointment to the United States Military Academy at West Point.

Frank didn't have the best educational background to compete for an academy appointment. Congressmen and senators appoint candidates to the Army, Navy and Air Force academies. Since each member of Congress can only have 5 constituents in an academy at one time, only one out of the 10 they are allowed to nominate each year to West Point is actually chosen. Naturally this makes the competition among applicants keen.

Frank had a poor academic background. In high school he had taken mostly shop courses and bypassed most mathematics, science, English and social science classes. In order to score well on the entrance exams, the young Marine attended the Naval Academy Preparatory School at Bainbridge, Maryland. Here he got the necessary training to win an appointment to the U. S. Military Academy at West Point.

At West Point, all freshmen or first year students are called plebes. As plebes, they are subjected to tremendous harassment by their upperclassmen. This harassment is actually part of their military training. The plebes learn to perform well while being harassed, a preparation for the days ahead when they may be called on to perform difficult duties while enduring the chaos and confusion of battle. Cadet Reasoner did so well his first that he was honored as the "Outstanding Plebe".

Frank's sports interests followed him to the academy. He was too short and light to play football, but played baseball his plebe year and wrestled and boxed all four years. Cadet Reasoner excelled at boxing. He was the brigade open boxing champion three of his four years at West Point. A broken nose prevented him from gaining the title his fourth year. Graduating from West Point in 1962, Frank left the Army to return to the Marines where he was commissioned as a second lieutenant.

By the Spring of 1965, America's involvement in Vietnam had gone beyond providing military "advisors". The United States was now deploying combat units. Frank Reasoner's battalion, the 3rd Reconnaissance Battalion, was ordered from Hawaii to Chu Lai, in the then Republic of Vietnam.

Frank first served as a platoon commander with Company B, 3rd Reconnaissance Battalion. After this unit was transferred to the 3rd Recon command post at Danang, Lt. Reasoner requested and was given command of Alpha Company, 3rd Recon. During a training exercise at China Beach, Frank intimated to a friend, Lieutenant Meyers that he didn't expect to go home alive. While many men with a premonition might seek safer duties, it was not the case with Frank. As company commander, he no longer had any obligation to take reconnaissance teams on patrol.

Nevertheless, on July 12, 1965, Lt. Reasoner and 1st Platoon, Company A, boarded helicopters at Danang for a ride to the town of Dai Loc.

The platoon commander was 2nd Lt. Bill Henderson. Other

members of the platoon included sixteen enlisted Marines, one Navy Corpsman, and a

Lieutenant Frank Reasoner

Vietnamese dog handler with his German Shepard. The mission of the platoon was to scout an area south of Danang where elements of the 9th Marine Regiment had encountered the enemy.

Arriving at Dai Loc, the platoon set up a relay station at the little fort manned and maintained by the Army of the Republic of Vietnam. Leaving behind two Marines to man the radio relay, the rest of the platoon moved up a dirt road out of the town. The road would take them through villages and rice fields, first to the west, then to the north.

As they were leaving town, Reasoner's platoon passed about fifty uniformed and armed Vietnamese, which the Marines took to be a local militia. The ARVN dog handler, however, tried to convince the Marines those troops were actually Viet Cong.

This was not a normal recon patrol. These men were used to being able to conceal themselves in heavy foliage. On this mission, however, they had to walk in the open, in daylight and through some not too friendly looking villages.

Approximately three hours into the patrol, while approaching the small village of An My, the platoon started receiving sniper fire. Lieutenant Henderson took half the platoon and went off in search of the sniper. Lt. Reasoner led the other half of the platoon into An My. As they entered, they noted that some villagers appeared to be hiding and some of the population missing. The team pushed on as a rainstorm hit and drenched the team. They passed a barrier fence of bamboo and cactus, crossing a ditch and came upon a graveyard with low, rounded grave mounds. Beyond the graveyard was a grave of trees and a small hill to the left.

Two of Reasoner's men spotted three Vietnamese in ponchos wearing helmets. These three Viet Cong spotted the Marines and ran toward the small hill. The Marines began to fire at them. The Viet Cong answered with a hail of machine gun fire from a fixed Soviet-made machine gun mounted on a tripod at the position on the hill. Soon additional fire poured in from the area near the machine gun. There were apparently more than three VC! The only cover the Marines had were the circular graves.

Since the enemy had the high ground, they were able to keep the Marines pinned down. Enjoying this advantage, the VC attempted to surround the Marines on the right and left flanks. The enemy began to inflict casualties. First they wounded the platoon sergeant, then Lance Corporal Hall, who had the M-79, which the team needed badly.

As the sun sank towards the horizon, Henderson's team reached Reasoner's. The Marines were now receiving fire from three directions, from an enemy that outnumbered them six or seven to one. The most formidable was the VC machine gunner who held the advantage of a superior position. Lt. Reasoner ordered Lt. Henderson to withdraw to the helicopter landing zone. As the Marines withdrew, assisting the wounded, Lt. Reasoner directed covering fire.

L.Cpl. Shockley, seeing that the other radioman's antenna had been shot off, realized Lt. Reasoner had no communications. Shockley scurried through the machine gun fire and managed to land next to the lieutenant without being hit. Unfortunately a VC bullet then found Shockley's elbow.

In an attempt to suppress the murderous fire from the well-placed, tripod-mounted machine gun, Lt. Reasoner repeatedly exposed himself to attack and killed at least two Viet Cong. One of Reasoner's men finally took out the deadly tripod-mounted gun with the M-79 grenade launcher; but the Viet Cong continued the assault with other automatic weapons. L.Cpl. Shockley was then wounded a second time. Lt. Reasoner ran for the wounded Marine; but Viet Cong bullets struck him, and he fell dead.

Five Marines traveling across the ground in a low crawl managed to reach the Lieutenant and recovered his body. Then they retrieved the wounded Shockley.

For his action, "In face of almost certain death...," Lt. Frank Reasoner was awarded the Congressional Medal of Honor. The Medal of was not the only recognition Lt. Reasoner received. The Marine Corps named the main home of the Reconnaissance Marines, Camp Reasoner. The Navy built and commissioned a frigate as the USS Reasoner. This ship served the Navy as part of the active fleet for 23 years. Back home, Kellogg High School honored their distinguished graduate with a wall mural of him, and establishing the McCoy-Reasoner Award. This award, named after Lt. Reasoner and an Air Force serviceman is presented each year to an outstanding athlete from the high school. Kootenai County, Idaho also maintains a picture of him in the courthouse at Coeur d'Alene.

Chapter 3 - Maurice Jacques – Hero of Ba To

Maurice Jacques was the oldest in a family with four children. As the oldest, he was the first to be given responsibility to help out with the household chores like cutting wood for the stove and feeding the chickens. One of Maurice's proud accomplishments as a child was the clubhouse he and about a dozen of his friends built. They dismantled an "abandoned" workmen's shed and rebuilt it in a vacant lot closer to their neighborhood.

Scrounging the neighborhood, the club members managed to find enough furniture to give their clubhouse some of the comforts of home.

Young Maurice learned wood lore from a grandfather who taught Maurice how to use an ax, build a fire, read a map, and use a compass. He applied these skills in the Boy

Scouts and earned quite a few merit badges. In school his favorite subjects were history and geography, which planted in him a desire to travel and see new places.

At the age of thirteen, Maurice Jacques became bored with high school and dropped out after completing 9th grade. At that age, and with limited education, he was forced to take up various jobs requiring manual labor. He worked on a relative's poultry farm and a neighboring vegetable farm. From there he moved on to working for a construction company, first as a laborer, then operating a jackhammer at $1.25 per hour. While working with this company, he met another worker named Whitey who had recently completed service with the Marine Corps. He told stories of Marine Corps Boot Camp and fighting the Japanese on the islands of Iwo Jima and Okinawa. These stories excited Maurice and convinced him to try the Marines himself. On July 12, 1948, at the age of 17 and with the consent of his parents he enlisted in the Marine Corps. A couple of days later, he was on a train headed for Parris Island, South Carolina.

Parris Island, where Marines from the Eastern United States receive basic training, has high humidity, heat, and all the biting and stinging pests associated with a swamp. In spite of the rigorous mental and physical demands of boot camp, Maurice Jacques excelled at training and scored the highest score of his platoon on the rifle range. At graduation, he received the rank of PFC. Only four others from the same platoon merited this rank upon graduation from boot camp.

After assignments in Guam and Hawaii, Maurice Jacques had his first taste of combat in Korea. Although the war started on June 25, 1950, when eight divisions of North Korean Communists crossed the 38th Parallel in an attempt to seize control of South Korea, Maurice Jacques didn't arrive in Korea until December 1952. By this time fighting in Korea had reached a stalemate with neither side being able to make any large gains against the other.

After the initial thrust southward, the North Koreans were repulsed when United Nations forces, led by U.S. Army and Marines arrived. The UN forces succeeded in pushing the North Koreans nearly to the Korean-Chinese border. China, however, unleashed huge numbers of troops against the UN forces, pushing them back down the peninsula of Korea again.

From March 26 through March 30, 1950, Maurice Jacques, now a sergeant and a squad leader, experienced some of the most intense fighting of the Korean War. It was on the 26th that the Chinese decided to mount a massive regimental assault against three hills, named Carson, Reno, and Vegas, after three Nevada Cities. These hills formed a semicircular series of outposts located just below the 38th parallel separating North and South Korea. The Chinese Communists wanted control of the hills because they would provide the Chinese with a commanding view of the land they desperately desired.

Sgt. Maurice Jacques's platoon occupied Reno from March 13 to 23rd. On the 23rd another platoon relieved them on the outpost, Reno. Sgt. Jacques and his platoon were ordered to occupy defensive positions along the main line of resistance, abbreviated MLR. This was a defensive line of troops, which ran east to the Samichan River. The Marines shared responsibility for defense of this line with South Korean Marines to their left along the line and the U.S. Army's 25th Infantry Division to the right. The portion of the line occupied by the Marines was apparently 5 miles long.

Five hundred yards from Sgt. Jacque's position on the MLR, and just before Reno, was a small hill dubbed Reno Block. A squad of Marines occupied this hill to help protect Reno from an attack from behind.

At first Sgt. Jacques's squad was only ordered to supply covering fire for a squad from Charlie Company as they moved up to occupy their position on Reno Block

At 7 p.m. on the 26th, the Chinese Communists opened

fire with artillery, mortars and machine guns all along the lines occupied by the 5th Marine Regiment. At the same time, they rained mortar and artillery shells down on the 5th Marine outposts of Reno and Carson. Shortly after the barrage began, Sgt. Jacques was ordered to take his squad and join a composite platoon to go forward and help reinforce the Marines fighting on Reno Block. As Sgt. Jacques describes it:

"This order was easier given than executed. The open ground in front of us was continuously being heaved skyward as artillery and heavy-mortar rounds slammed to earth. With no lull to the number of incoming rounds, there was little time to organize our movement. We understood the urgency of moving to help support Reno Block, but it was a matter of heroic individual effort to get there. Having returned from Reno only three days earlier, we knew the closer we got to reaching Reno Block, the closer we would get to a minefield we had encountered during our return to the MLR. The enemy mines, hidden under snow, had been revealed after several days of torrential warm spring rain. The exposed antitank "box-mines" had been laid months earlier in the narrow avenues of approach and now presented a significant problem to anyone who dared to approach the area.

I had started to move off the MLR, with DeLuca, Fuller, Davis and Augire right behind me, and Lopez, Fry, Sutton, and Signoski were in trace of them. But by the time we had moved less than three hundred yards, the number of incoming artillery rounds had increased, making progress virtually impossible. We could do little more than stay in the cold mud, hoping we would not fall victim to the continuous barrage.

By 2200 hours, my squad had been decimated from incoming artillery, mortar and small-arms fire. DeLuca was dead, killed by shrapnel, as were Augire, Signoski and Davis. Sutton had been seriously wounded, along with Lopez. Miraculously, only Fry and myself has escaped being hit. Sometime close to 2300, Fry and I and half a dozen Marines of the platoon were joined by a squad of Marines from Item Company, 3/5, who had been in reserve and directed to shift from their positions on our right flank and come to the aid of those Marines still holding out on Reno Block. But despite our attempts to move up to the Block, we could get no closer than several hundred yards from it. We were caught in the middle of a no-man's-land crisscrossed with enemy machine-gun fire, able to stay alive only by killing the approaching Chinese soldiers silhouetted by the light of flares, and by not daring to move and expose ourselves. At that moment, a Marine's world was no greater than the five yards of the cold muddy ground around him. In the distance we could see that the Chinese had begun their assault on Reno and were using flamethrowers to push Marines back toward the top of the hill." [1]

Ten minutes after the artillery and mortar attack began, thirty-five hundred Chinese followed the assault against all the 5th Marine Regiment positions. The Chinese outnumbered the outposts like Reno by twenty to one. Soon the Marines on Carson were fighting off their attackers with bayonets, knives, rifle butts and bare fists. As reinforcements were dispatched to assist Carson, the Chinese unexpectedly began to back off from Carson in order to concentrate on Reno and Vegas, which were further away from the main Marine forces. By 10:00 p.m., the Communists had pushed their way into the trenches on Reno and Vegas, forcing the defending Marines into caves on the hill. By midnight, the Chinese Communists were in control of Vegas and Reno. From Reno they were in position to prevent Marines from retaking the hill and rescuing its remaining defenders. By this time, only five of the original Marine defenders had not been killed.

At Vegas, by 3:00 a.m. on March 27th, a Marine relief platoon managed to get within two hundred yards of that outpost before discovering the enemy was in control of it also. At this time the Marine commanders pulled their relief troops back to the MLR, in favor of launching a coordinated attack at dawn. From the beginning of the assault eight hours earlier, casualties had been heavy on both sides; but the Chinese suffered the worst with an estimated 600 killed or wounded.

At dawn the Chinese pulled back and the Marines were able to locate their killed and wounded and move back to the MLR. At this time the commanding officer of the 3rd Battalion, 5th Marine Regiment organized the remnants of the 1st, 3rd, and 5th Battalions into a single battalion to prepare for a new assault. The orders were to draw fresh ammunition and try again to get to Reno Block. At this point, Sergeant Jacques discovered that "… a bullet had cut a deep crease across the top of my pack, missing my head by only a few inches". [2]

Through the 27th and 28th, the Marines contested the Chinese over the hill, Vegas. The battle raged with aircraft, tanks, artillery and mortars supporting the troops attempting to regain Vegas. The Chinese battled back with murderous, continuous, small arms fire and grenade bursts. By 11:07 p.m., the Marines finally recaptured Vegas.

From captured Chinese prisoners the Marines learned that the Chinese 358th Regiment was trying to occupy Vegas and Reno before an expected United Nations spring offensive could be launched. These two positions overlooked important supply routes. Sure enough, during the night of 28-29 March, the Chinese counter attacked; but without success. While this was going on, Sgt. Jacques and his squad of men were dug in along the MLR, keeping a steady stream of small arms fire concentrated on enemy silhouettes moving about less than 100 yards in front of them.

On the morning of March 30th, the Chinese finally gave up Vegas for good. This five-day battle for the outposts named after Nevada cities left Sgt. Jacques questioning the wisdom of his decision to seek out a combat role in the Marine Corps.

In 1964, after assignments that included competing on a Marine Corps rifle team and service as a drill instructor, Sgt. Jacques decided to take up a new challenge – becoming a Recon Marine. He went through parachute training at Fort Benning, Georgia. Then Maurice went to scuba school in San Diego, California. Having received his jump and diver qualifications, Maurice Jacques became a full-fledged member of 1st Force Reconnaissance Company. In February 1965 he was promoted to Gunnery Sergeant. Now a fully professional Marine, combat seasoned and highly trained, Maurice Jacques was about to meet his greatest challenge yet, at a place called Ba To.

Gunny Jacques and 1st Force Reconnaissance Company conducted their first patrols in South Vietnam in the summer of 1965. He did encounter the Viet Cong on a occasion; but the toughest patrol was yet to come.

On November 27, 1965, Maurice Jacques' platoon was taken to A-106, located in the jungle near the village of Ba To. This area was surrounded by mountains and infested with Viet Cong and North Vietnamese regulars. U.S. Army Special Forces (Green Berets) ran the camp; but local South Vietnamese forces known as CIDG's (Civilian Irregular Defense Group) assisted in the defense of the camp.

Gunny Jacques

The Marines' assignment was to find the routes the enemy used to move troops about in order to mount offensives in attempts to control the local population. They were also directed to find and monitor a large enemy staging area, an underground hospital, and several high speed trails.

On December 14, 1965, Gunny Jacques leading 16 Marines from his platoon, accompanied a company of sixty-one CIDG soldiers lead by a South Vietnamese Army Lieutenant and Sergeant West from Army Special Forces. They left the Special Forces camp to set up an outpost near Vic

Liem. When they reached the outpost, Gunny Jacques sent out his teams to conduct reconnaissance. His teams discovered large groups of uniformed North Vietnamese soldiers carrying AK-47 and SKS rifles, enemy hootches, recent cooking fires, and the locations of enemy observation and listening posts.

On the evening of December 16th at about 7 p.m., two well-aimed 60 mm mortar rounds impacted on the northwestern side of the hill occupied by GySgt Jacques and the rest of the recon forces. Shrapnel from these rounds killed the lieutenant leading the CIDG forces, and destroyed his radio. Appearing with the mortar rounds, were streaks of green machine-gun tracers and accompanying bullets. Staff Sergeant West fell, being mortally wounded, with his radio smashed, leaving the rest of the troops without communications.

In the next two hours, another estimated 100 mortar rounds pounded their position. Then, 150 to 200 North Vietnamese soldiers advanced toward them. The enemy managed to segregate the defending CIDG forces into small groups. The NVA assaulted with voluminous automatic weapons fire and dozens of hand grenades. As the defenders returned fire, in the confusion of the night, the possibility of mistaking friendly for enemy targets became a reality. Through his interpreter, Gunny Jacques learned that the voices around them were shouting in a distinct North Vietnamese dialect, directing their troops and coordinating the assault. Gunny Jacques wondered if they hadn't been betrayed by members of the CIDG unit, who were Communists sympathizers, and had probably led the attacking forces past the listening posts.

Maurice quickly set about preparing a defense with his Marines, and those few men from the CIDG group he could "grab and hold in place." [3] Gunny Jacques sent Lance Corporal Moore to find out why the CIDG mortar team wasn't returning fire on the NVA. Moore found the team had run off. He managed to find one of them hiding in the grass, but, not speaking Vietnamese, he couldn't get the CIDG soldier to help. When Moore went to unwrap a mortar round, the Vietnamese ran off.

Gunny Jacques ran over to assist Moore with firing the mortar; but when the NVA saw the two of them were ready to fire, they dropped half a dozen rounds on top of them. Shrapnel from the incoming rounds seriously wounded Moore. Jacques called for the Corpsman, Doc Haston, but the enemy mortars had also wounded him badly. Gunny Jacques rushed to him and tried to stop his bleeding. The mortar shrapnel had torn a large hole in the Corpsman's chest. Gunny Jacques longed to give him a drug to kill the pain; but was afraid it would render the corpsman unable to walk. With casualties mounting, the fewer who needed to be carried, the better. He bandaged Doc Haston's wounds the best he could and carried him to where the rest of the group had gathered.

The Gooks now had a good fix on the Marine's position and Gunny Jacques know they had to move if they were to survive. He called for the rest of the Marines in his platoon to join up with his group. Three Marines, Sergeant Akioks, Sergeant Blanton, and Corporal Lynch were the only ones able to respond and Akioks was wounded! Sergeant Blanton assisted Gunny Jacques in covering the withdrawal of the rest of the men as they moved over the crest of the hill and into a banana grove.

Suddenly Maurice Jacques felt a blow to his upper chest, which knocked him backwards, followed by a burning pain radiating from his neck. Because it was dark and raining he couldn't assess how badly he was bleeding. He tried to keep moving; but the taste of blood filled his mouth. He realized he'd been hit in the throat and the wound was serious. He began to choke, but managed to keep breathing by swallowing his blood. He used the fingers of his left hand to keep his shirt pressed against the wound. Then he grabbed his M-2 carbine rifle and crawled off in the direction of the banana grove to join the others.

When he had the opportunity to take care of himself, he discovered that the bullet which had struck him in the neck, had ricocheted off his first aid kit before striking the neck. He surmised that, had the AK-47 round hit him directly, he would have been killed.

His throat swelled, and he had trouble speaking. But knew if he couldn't give orders, Sergeant Blanton wouldn't be able to help him. When GySgt Jacques joined the rest or the group, he realized they couldn't move down into the stream below them because they had seen the muzzle flashes of the enemy machine guns near the water's edge. To complicate matters, the North Vietnamese now had begun a systematic search for escaping and wounded soldiers from the hill.

Since the NVA had to physically shift their Machine guns to get at the Marines, it gave them extra time to find deeper cover in the grove. At this time, Sergeant Baker and Corporal Young got separated from the rest of the group. Using banana leaves, Gunny Jacques and his mobile troops covered themselves and the wounded. Then they set up a hasty defense. They were convinced it would only be a matter of time before the NVA searchers found their trail and came looking for them.

As they hid, they heard the NVA discover the bodies of Lance Corporal Brown and Corporal Joy. They killed Joy but forced Brown to his feet, and led him away from the hilltop. Brown, already wounded, looked for a chance to escape.

When the single file line of men hit a narrow portion of the trail, he dove into the dense vegetation. With the NVA sporadically shooting into the bush, Brown rolled away and ended up near Gunny Jacques' group in the banana grove. The Marines grabbed the surprised Brown, pulled him in with their group, and started to move down the hill again. Suddenly a searchlight illuminated the area. Apparently the NVA had brought the searchlight along for the attack, to spot and kill any survivors. This they proceeded to do. Any South Vietnamese soldier or Marine they located with the light they would shoot to kill. All Gunny Jacques and his group could do was remain motionless in the banana grove and pray that aerial spotter planes might assist them at daybreak.

The first light of morning brought no hope for an emergency extraction. First, they crawled farther west; but were met with a hail of enemy gunfire. They tried a different direction; but the NVA started firing again. This time, however, the NVA were firing at CIDG survivors who were not part of the Gunny's group. Jacques moved his people toward another section of the ridgeline and away from the hill. After progressing about three thousand yards, they stopped for a rest. After putting his men in the standard 360-degree defense, he heard the sound of brush breaking nearby.

Exhausted, Maurice Jacques, satisfied himself he had done everything possible to get his men away from the NVA. He pulled his last magazine of .30 caliber rounds from its pouch and loaded it into his carbine. As he prepared to fire, when the first gook target presented himself, one of the CIDG soldiers with the Gunny's group placed the fingers of one hand over his mouth, gesturing the Gunny to be quiet, then gestured him not to shoot.

They were surprised when two CIDG soldiers appeared. The soldiers had managed to survive the night and happened to cross the same trail. Now the group, reinforced by two more, moved from the resting place. They soon encountered a high-speed trail running in the direction they wished to travel. Recon Marines were taught to stay off such trails because they often were bobby trapped or the enemy waited in an ambush. Maurice Jacques, however, decided to risk it. It was important to distance themselves from their pursuers.

Several hundred yards down the trail; they heard movement behind them. They spread out in a hasty defense; but soon discovered Sergeant Baker and Corporal Young coming up the trail. Gunny Jacques was thrilled to see they were alive and armed! To the Gunny, the addition of two Marine riflemen meant the difference between the team getting back alive or not returning at all.

The top priority now was to return to the safety of the Special Forces camp without running into the NVA. Gunny Jacques put two of the CIDG soldiers and Sergeant Baker up front. He reasoned that if the NVA should see two Vietnamese approaching on their trail, it might just give the team enough time to break through an ambush. With cover from dense fog and monsoon rainstorm the team was able to move more rapidly along the trail without detection. Before long, however they found themselves on a portion of the trail with unmanned fighting holes alongside it. They were walking through the assembly area, which the North Vietnamese had used to stage their men before their attack!

At 2:00 p.m. on December 17, the nine-man team finally walked through the perimeter wire at Ba To. By then, the Gunny had lost his voice due to the swelling from the bullet wound in his neck. They were taken directly to the Special Forces aid station for initial treatment. An hour later Doc Haston, Sergeant Akioke, and Gunny Jacques were medevaced to the U.S. Navy medical battalion at Chu Lai.

The doctor at Chu Laiwho attended Gunny Jacques told him he was a very lucky Marine. The doctor explained:

> "That bullet passed through a small portion of your trachea which has no bones near it. A fraction of an inch either way, Gunny Jacques, and you would probably have drowned in your own blood. After the swelling goes down, and if there's no infection, you'll be fine and can return to your unit." [4]

By January 1966, however, Maurice Jacques was back on patrol again with 1st Force Recon.

Maurice Jacques left Vietnam on December 18, 1966; but returned again in December 1967. This time he undertook the duties of 1st Sergeant for Echo Company, 1st Reconnaissance Battalion. Again he managed to mix it up with the NVA; but survived to leave Vietnam in January 1969. He returned again in December 1969. After duty with Mike Company, 3rd Battalion, 1st Marine Regiment and 1st Force Reconnaissance Company, Maurice Jacques became 1st Sergeant of Bravo Company, 1st Reconnaissance Battalion. In January 1971, 1st Sgt. Maurice Jacques left Vietnam for the last time. He had spent forty-three months of duty in Vietnam; but his closest brush with death occurred at Ba To.

[1] From *Sergeant Major, U.S. Marines* pages 113-114
[2] From *Sergeant Major, U.S. Marines* page 122.
[3] From *Sergeant Major, U.S. Marines* page 255.
[4] From *Sergeant Major, U.S. Marines* page 262
.

Chapter 4 - Skibbe, McVey & Rathmell - Leaving No Man Behind

It has long been a tradition in the Marine Corps that every effort is made to ensure no Marine is left behind whether dead or alive. This chapter tells the story of three Reconnaissance Marines who died in this effort.

On March 2, 1970, a seven-man reconnaissance team from "C" Company, 1st Reconnaissance Battalion, was inserted into an area about 10 miles northwest of the city of An Hoa. The patrol leader was 2nd Lt. David W. Skibbe and this was his first reconnaissance patrol.

David W, Skibbe was born October 22, 1946. He grew up in Des Plaines, Illinois. His father, William Skibbe was a World War II veteran and a retired Captain from the U.S. Army. Even as a child, David Skibbe was a leader. Among the children in his neighborhood, he was kind of an organizer and decided what games the kids would play. David was also ambitious. He had his own paper route to make "pocket money". One day, while delivering papers he noticed that a house in the country was selling puppies. He bought a black Labrador who he named "Lady". He trained this dog in obedience and retrieving dummy birds.

David was also a Boy Scout and an Explorer Scout. In high school he sported a red Corvette. He played baseball and basketball and ran cross-country. David's love of the outdoors lead him to get a degree in forestry from the University of Illinois in 1969. At the University of Illinois, he was a member of the Beta Sigma Psi fraternity and participated in Naval Reserve Officer Training Corps. During the 1967-1968 academic year he was Battalion Commander of the NROTC. He was Outstanding NROTC Midshipman from Naval Order of the United States in 1967, and awarded Meritorious Achievement from the Marine Corps Association in 1968. He completed USMC Basic School with a Superior Achievement award and was commissioned as a 2nd Lieutenant in 1969.

On this mission, Lt. Skibbe's assistant patrol leader was Corporal Larry Gifford, a veteran Marine, who had been in Vietnam since September 11, 1969. Walking point was Lance Corporal Steven Plunkett. Plunkett had been in Vietnam since May 1969.

At about 4:30 p.m., the team was moving south, southeast on a high speed trail on a ridgeline when Plunkett spotted two Viet Cong wearing black pajama tops and light colored khaki shorts. The VC were carrying rifles slung over their shoulders. The enemy spotted the recon team at approximately the same time. The VC opened fire with automatic weapons. The recon team returned fire and jumped off to the side of the trail. The enemy continued to fire, striking Corporal Gifford in the knee, thumb and head; then broke contact.

Lt. Skibbe

Lt. Skibbe administered first aid to Corporal Gifford; but then they were attacked again by an estimated five more of the enemy. This time, Lt. Skibbe was hit. The team returned fire with unknown results. The enemy continued to fire for another three minutes, then broke contact. The team radioed for an air observer.

About 4:45 p.m., air observers, designated as Hostage Six and Scarface arrived above the team's position. The AO's laid down supporting fire. At approximately 6:30 p.m., Ch-46 transport helicopters and helicopter gunships arrived above the team. One Ch-46 lowered the jungle penetrator to hoist out the wounded. Larry Gifford was hoisted out without incident and the penetrator lowered to extract Lt. Skibbe. The team hooked on Lt. Skibbe and used safety straps to insure the Lieutenant wouldn't fall off.

On the first try, the cable got caught in the canopy; but the team broke the cable loose. The team then observed Lt. Skibbe penetrate the canopy and he was approximately 100 feet off the ground when the team started to put on their gear. The extract ladder was lowered to the team. They scrambled up it, hooked on, and were extracted.

At this time the team was confident Lt. Skibbe had made it aboard the helicopter. It wasn't until the helicopter with the team aboard set down at An Hoa, that they learned Lt. Skibbe hadn't successfully been extracted. In the confusion of the emergency extract, Lt. Skibbe was lost. When the team and their company commander, Captain Lavoy McVey had a chance to sort things out, the following facts were ascertained.

Lt. Skibbe suffered a "penetrating wound of the lower right leg, breaking the fibula 2 inches above the ankle leaving an open fracture," according to the team Corps man, HM3 McLynn. Shortly after McLynn administered treatment, the team put Lt. Skibbe on the jungle penetrator. The team was only able to observe the Lieutenant until he cleared the canopy of the jungle, which was some 30-40 feet in height.

Meanwhile, from the helicopter into which Skibbe was being hoisted, Captain McVey, the medical officer, helicopter pilots and crewman, watched Skibbe's ascent until he reached about 20 feet from the chopper (100 ft. or more above ground). At that moment, the hoist cable suddenly snapped and Skibbe fell to the ground, although those on the helicopter couldn't see what happened to him after he disappeared into the foliage below.

The pilot of the recovery helicopter immediately contracted the team on the ground by radio and received the message, "Yes, he's okay." The pilot understood this to mean that the team found Skibbe. The pilot, therefore, swung about, and lowered the extract ladder for the team. The Marines climbed on, unaware that Skibbe had fallen close by, and were hoisted into the air for the return trip to An Hoa.

Both CH-46 helicopters returned to the area where Lt. Skibbe had gone down. At this time, they attempted to insert Captain McVey, the Charlie Company Commander to search for Lt. Skibbe.

Captain McVey came from Lamar, Colorado. He graduated from Lamar Union High School in 1956. Lavoy McVey loved the outdoors and spent many hours hunting in the foothills of the Rocky Mountains. His love of the outdoors led him to join the Boy Scouts, and, upon graduation from high school, he enlisted in the Marine Corps. He served as an infantryman until 1965. In 1965, Sergeant McVey was accepted into Officer Candidate School (OCS) and, upon completing OCS, he was commissioned as a 2nd Lt. In 1966, he went to Vietnam for his first tour.

In 1970, now a Captain, and assigned as Commanding Officer of Charlie Company, 1st Recon Battalion, he had been on long-range reconnaissance patrols with the men from his Company. On March 2, 1970, he'd accompanied the helicopters sent to extract his team, *Thin Man*, who had come in contact with the enemy. Upon learning Lt. Skibbe was unaccounted for, he insisted on returning to the extract site. Due to the impossibility of landing a helicopter in the area, Captain McVey volunteered to be lowered by the jungle penetrator, the same technique, which resulted in the loss of Lt. Skibbe.

It was now dark and an aircraft had dropped flares to illuminate the area where Lt. Skibbe had been lost. While the helicopter was hovering over the area, and Captain McVey was going down on the jungle penetrator, the flares went out. Below all was darkness.

Since the helicopter crew had no reference to their altitude above the jungle in the dark, the pilot started a climb and directed the crew chief to reel in the hoist. The pilot planned to try again after illumination could be restored.

As the crew chief extended his hand to pull Captain

McVey in, the cable snapped and the Captain disappeared

l   **Captain McVey**

into the darkness below. After this, the pilot had no choice but to abort this mission, with the idea that a recovery team could be inserted at first light. A search was conducted later; but neither the body of Captain McVey or Lt. Skibbe were found.

Lt. Skibbe was awarded the Navy Cross for his actions on March 2, 1970. The award citation describes his actions as follows:

"For extraordinary heroism while serving as a Platoon Commander with Company C, First Reconnaissance Battalion, First Marine Division in connection with combat operations against the enemy in the Republic of Vietnam. On 2 March 1970, while Second Lt. Skibbe was leading a patrol deep in enemy-controlled territory, the team came under a heavy volume of fire from a large hostile force.

During the initial moments of the engagement, Second Lt. Skibbe observed a wounded man fall in a forward position, and unhesitatingly placed himself between the casualty and enemy soldiers to deliver intense covering fire which forced the enemy momentarily to break contact and enabled the Marines to move the wounded man to a more secure location.

While the radio operator was requesting air support, the lieutenant was severely wounded in the ankle. Although suffering intense pain and unable to walk, he nevertheless skillfully directed the bombing and strafing runs of supporting aircraft with such accuracy that the hostile soldiers broke contact and retreated, thereby enabling a medical evacuation helicopter to come to a safe hover overhead.

As Second Lt. Skibbe was being hoisted toward the aircraft, the hoist apparatus sustained a malfunction, and he was mortally injured when he fell to the ground. His heroic and determined actions throughout this mission contributed significantly to the defeat of the numerically superior enemy force. By his courage, valiant leadership, and unwavering devotion to duty in the face of grave personal danger, Second Lt. Skibbe upheld the highest traditions of the Marine Corps and of the United States Naval Service. He gallantly gave his life in the service of his country."

Captain McVey received a Silver Star for his effort to rescue or recover the body of Lt. Skibbe.

For their actions on the same patrol that 2nd day of March, team member Larry Gifford was awarded the Bronze Star Medal, as was Steven Plunkett; and Ray Jones the Navy Commendation Medal.

A little more than a month later, the "jungle penetrator" hoist was to claim the life of yet another fine Marine Officer.

Henry Porter Rathmell grew up in the country. His father served in the Marine Corps during World War II; and was probably the reason Henry chose to serve years later. Henry started his education at a two-room country school in the village of Pennsdale, Pennsylvania. This school only provides education through 6th grade, so, when the time came, Henry had to transfer to the junior/senior high school at Muncy, Pa.

Henry also loved the outdoors. He joined the Boy Scouts and stayed with them until he had an opportunity to become a counselor at Vagabond Ranch in Granby, Colorado. While in the Boy Scouts, his troop participated in a 50-mile hike. Fifty-mile hikes were something of a fad in the early 1960's. This was because President John. F. Kennedy resurrected an old order once given by President Theodore "Teddy" Roosevelt ordering the Marines to complete a 50-mile hike as part of their training. Anyway, Henry performed the best on the hike because he was used to hiking about the hills of Pennsylvania. Henry's father taught him to hunt and fish and how to use a rifle. In Colorado, He learned mountain climbing, a skill, which would serve him well later.

In high school, Henry made the honor roll; but was only an average athlete. He sprouted to 6'-4", played tight end on the football team, and center on the basketball team. He continued to play basketball his freshman year at Colgate

College after high school.

In 1968 Henry Rathmell graduated from Colgate with a degree in Geology. At this time, the war in Vietnam was at its peak. The Marines in Vietnam had just successfully beat back a vicious offensive by the NVA/Viet Cong, which coincided with the Vietnamese New Year (TET). They had also successfully held the outpost of Khe Sanh, despite being surrounded by a much larger force of the enemy.

By this time, however, the Vietnam War was becoming unpopular in the United States. Protests against the war occurred, and many draft eligible males sought the protection of college to avoid induction into the Army. Henry Porter could have gone on to Graduate school or joined some other branch of the military than the Marine Corps; but he desired to be the best so he headed off to Quantico, Virginia and Marine Officer Candidate School.

Following his initial training and commissioning as a 2nd Lt., he went to the Basic School (TBS). Here Lt. Rathmell excelled and was named to the Commanding General's Honor List. His next assignment was to attend U.S. Army's School of Infantry Ranger Course at Fort Benning, Georgia. Here he graduated as the Distinguished Honor Graduate (1st among 230 students).

With this ranger training under his belt, Lt. Rathmell was sent to Vietnam and assigned to the 3rd Reconnaissance Battalion, 3rd Marine Division. Here he completed six long-range reconnaissance patrols; the 3rd Marine Division was soon ordered to Okinawa as part of the effort to reduce the number of troops in Vietnam. Lt. Rathmell, however, longed to remain with Marines in Vietnam. He sought and received a reassignment to the 1st Reconnaissance Battalion. He was assigned to Delta Company.

During a patrol in March of 1970, Lt. Rathmell was on a team that discovered a cave system loaded with enemy supplies. These the reconnaissance team destroyed.

Lieutenant Rathmell

On the 12th of April 1970, LT. Rathmell led a
reconnaissance team in an effort to recover the body of a
Marine pilot whose plane had crashed. Lt. Rathmell was
inserted first. Immediately, however, he came in contact with
the enemy. Lt. Rathmell signaled the helicopters not to land
the rest of the team. Both of the CH-46 helicopters headed
back for 1st Reconnaissance Battalion. A Staff Sergeant on one
of the helicopters, however, convinced the pilot to return for
Lt. Rathmell.

When the helicopter returned, its crew lowered the
"jungle penetrator" for Lt. Rathmell. But as Lt. Rathmell was
hoisted out of the jungle the cable broke and he disappeared
into the jungle below. His body was recovered, and returned

to the United States for burial. For his actions on April 12, Lt. Rathmell was awarded the Bronze Star Medal.

Chapter 5 - *Rush Act* - The Patrol that Did Not Return

John F. Stockman reported to Marine Corps Boot Camp at Parris Island on September 21, 1966. A twenty-three year old from Marcus Hook, Pa, he was about to embark on a distinguished career in the Marine Corps. After boot camp and basic infantry training, John Stockman reported for duty on March 10, 1967 with Company D, 3rd Reconnaissance Battalion, 3rd Marine Division in Vietnam. Throughout the remainder of this tour he participated in no less than 13 operations against the enemy forces in South Vietnam.

On March 24, 1968, he left Vietnam for San Francisco; but in November 1968 he was back in Vietnam. This time he was a scout with 1st Battalion, 4th Marine Regiment, 3rd Marine

Division. Nevertheless, he managed to get back to Company D, 3rd Recon Bn by December 5, 1968. There he remained until September of 1969, when he was released from active service.

But for John Stockman, the Marine Corps, and, in particular, recon, was a way of life. So, by October 1970 he was in Bravo Company, 1st Reconnaissance Battalion.

On May 29, 1969, Fernando Villasana reported for recruit training at Marine Corps Recruit Depot, San Diego, California. He was a young man of 19 years and had left his home in El Paso, Texas. After training in infantry and reconnaissance, he found himself in January 1970 with Delta Company, 1st Reconnaissance Battalion. When Delta Company was disbanded in 1970, Villasana was transferred to Bravo Company. During his time in Delta and Bravo Company he participated in a total of 25 long-range reconnaissance patrols. He also participated in "Lynch Law", a long-range combat raid in Que Nam Province, RVN.

Russell Daniels became a Navy Corpsman. At age 19 he reported to Navy boot camp on San Diego, California. After boot camp, he attended training at the Naval Hospital in San Diego and at the Naval Hospital in Philadelphia, Pa. In February 1970 he reported for duty as a Corpsman with 5th Marine Regiment, 1st Marine Division, but in July 1970 he was transferred to Bravo Company, 1st Reconnaissance Battalion. "Doc Daniels" as he was known, had a mischievous sense of humor. Not unlikely to play a practical joke on one of his buddies; he maintained a good sense of humor when the joke was on him.

Bravo Company, for instance, had a Company dog named Willy. Now no one knew what kind of dog Willy was. He bore the main characteristics of a Golden Retriever, with blond fur and all; but it was very unlikely Willy was purebred anything. Anyway, Willy ran around the company area; but it wasn't unusual for Willy to wander off – particularly at night. When Willy wandered off at night he often went to the rice paddies outside the Battalion compound. The Vietnamese fertilized the rice paddies with manure of all kinds so when Willy came back from a night down there, he often smelled rather rank.

Willy

One day Willy, fresh from a night in the paddies, decided to plant himself on Doc Daniels cot. Doc Daniels entered the hootch. Spotting Willy, he decided to give the dog a big hug. Almost immediately, Doc Daniels was repulsed by the stench and backed off. Doc's roommates were amused by his reaction. Doc ordered Willy out of the hootch.

Robert Tucker joined the Marine Corps in April of 1969 at the age of 20. He came from Abbyville, Kansas. From boot camp and Infantry Training Regiment he went to Basic Infantry Training School at Camp Pendleton, California. In July of 1970 he was assigned to Bravo Company, 1st Recon Bn, soon to become one of a team that would never be forgotten.

He participated in "Lynch Law", the same long-range combat raid as Villasana.

Charles Pope, born in Independence, Missouri, reported to boot camp in San Diego at the age of 18. After Basic Infantry Training School at Camp Pendleton, California, he found himself in Bravo Company, 1st Recon Bn. by March 1970. Here he participated in "Lynch Law" as well as 23 long-range reconnaissance patrols.

At age nineteen, Gary Hudson, another Missourian, left his home in Joplin, Missouri to join the Marine Corps. After boot camp at San Diego, Ca, he underwent training as a radio operator and July 1, 1970 he reported for duty at 1st Reconnaissance Battalion. After two months training at H&S Company, he was assigned to Bravo Company as a field radio operator. Between September 4, 1970 and November 18, 1970, he served as a primary radioman on 10 long-range reconnaissance patrols and an attack on a fortified enemy bunker complex in the Que Son Mountains. Service, for which he earned the Bronze Star.

At age nineteen, David Delozier joined the Marine Corps and started training at Parris Island, South Carolina in September of 1969. For David it was a short trip from boot camp to Vietnam. By March 12, 1970, he was a member of Bravo Company, 1st Reconnaissance Battalion. Between March 11 and 18 November 1970, he participated in 24 long-range reconnaissance patrols and "Lynch Law, a long-range combat raid.

David Delozier came from Altoona, Pennsylvania. It was a little railroad town where people didn't talk a lot about the war in Vietnam. In high school, the 5'-8", 160 lb. Delozier, excelled in football and participated in track. A bright lad, with youthful good looks, he was also popular among his fellow students and his senior year they elected him class president. David also managed to score David Delozier came from Altoona, Pennsylvania. It was a little railroad town where people didn't talk a lot about the war in Vietnam. In high school, the 5'-8", 160 lb. Delozier, excelled in football and participated in track. A bright lad, with youthful good looks, he was also popular among his fellow students and his senior year they elected him class president. David also managed to score scholarships to college; but left after his first year to join the Marine Corps. He chose the Corps because it was the toughest branch of the services.

A couple of months into his Vietnam tour, David's father had a heart attack. While home on emergency leave, he and a friend, Bill Teufel went to visit a cousin who was a student at Kent State University. At this time, Kent State was a hot bed of protest against the Vietnam War. In fact, in May 1970 the students organized a demonstration against the war on campus. Things got out of hand, and soon four students lost their lives because the students assaulted National Guard troops, who were sent there to protect people and property. Nevertheless, David Delozier returned to resume his duties in Vietnam, with no less a devotion to country and Corps.

In November 1970, Lt. Col. William Leftwich Jr. commanded the 1st Reconnaissance Battalion. He was a 34 year-old Marine Officer who had graduated from the U.S. Naval Academy in 1953.

William Leftwich came from a wealthy family in Memphis, Tennessee. In high school he was the captain of the football team and became an excellent tennis player. Bill could probably have afforded to attend any college of his choice; but he chose the Naval Academy instead.

In 1949, he entered the Academy as a Midshipman. This 5'-10 ½" tall, good- looking, and young man soon won the admiration of his fellow students. Always maintaining good physical condition, Leftwich played tennis, squash and football. He rose to the position of Head of the Brigade. Always displaying his Tennessee friendliness, he won friends easily among the other Midshipman. Two of his good friends,

Ross Perot and Bob Bell, would become notable as a Presidential candidate and Admiral years later. Upon graduation, William Leftwich chose to serve as an officer in the U.S. Marine Corps.

By March 1965, William Leftwich had obtained the rank of Major and was serving in Vietnam as an advisor to Task Force Alpha, a Vietnamese Marine Brigade. Major Leftwich demonstrated his courage and leadership skills on a mission with the brigade March 9, 1965. He first arranged for very close air support. The plan was bold, because he requested that the air crews fire extra close to the front lines and to fake additional attacks as the Vietnamese Marines assaulted the enemy positions. Major Leftwich also planned a route of march, based on last minute intelligence which prevented the Vietnamese Marines from running into a massive ambush. When the assault began, Major Leftwich moved to the front of the assaulting force. Under heavy fire, he directed the air support during the assault. Shouting and shooting point-blank at the enemy, he lead the Vietnamese troops past the outward Viet Cong defenses and to within forty meters of the crest of a hill overlooking Hoai An. Machine gun bullets struck him in the back, cheek and nose. Nevertheless, a comrade fell, mortally wounded; and Major Leftwich rushed to aid him. Although bleeding profusely himself, Major Leftwich shunned assistance, and medical evacuation, until he could call for additional air strikes and let the Task Force Commander know what was happening. For his bravery during this action, he was awarded the Navy Cross.

After recovering from his wounds, William Leftwich became an Aide to the Undersecretary of the Navy. Being a man of action, however, he left the cushy staff officer life behind to return to Vietnam. He first took the position of Battalion Commander, 2nd Battalion, 1st Marine Regiment on May 16, 1970. While Commander of the 2/1, Lt. Col. Leftwich organized a surprise raid on enemy bunkers, which resulted in the elimination of three high-ranking Viet Cong officers.

On September 13, 1970, he took over as the Commander of the 1st Reconnaissance Battalion. By this time, the Battalion had been reduced from 5 companies of reconnaissance scouts to two. President Nixon had ordered the reduction of troops as part of his policy to withdraw American forces in Vietnam. The President felt that the Vietnamese should increasingly bear the responsibility to defend their country. In March 1970, the control of military operations in the five Northern Provinces was transferred from the Marine Corps to the U.S. Army with the view to eventually transferring command to the Army of the Republic of Vietnam.

To make the most effective use of his recon marines, Lt. Col. Leftwich turned the responsibility for security of the four observation posts to infantry units and reorganized the two remaining letter companies. The reorganized battalion provided him 24 reconnaissance teams, an average of 12 of which were in the bush at any given time.

On November 10, 1970, Corporal Stockman led Corpsman Daniels and five other Marines off Landing Zone Ranch House to conduct a reconnaissance patrol. The team's call sign was *Rush Act*. The members of this team would never return.

As Corporal Stockman led his team through their assigned grid of jungle, they soon discovered the enemy had been busy about their business. First, there was the discovery of the LAAW. LAAW stands for light anti-tank assault weapon. Designed and manufactured in the United States, the mere presence of such a weapon in enemy territory evokes suspicion. Someone, however, placed this one at a 45-degree angle on the insert landing zone. Apparently the guerrillas intended to use it on a helicopter landing on the LZ. Believing that the LAAW might be booby trapped, the team didn't attempt to disassemble it.

About four in the afternoon of the next day, the team came on a recently constructed trail about 18" wide. The next day came the bonanza, they discovered an enemy village. The village was composed of six hootches with thatched roofs. Nearby were rice paddies where four enemy soldiers were located. One of these was of military age; but that one wasn't working. The team spotted two additional military-aged men entering the hootches. Later that day, more men arrived. This time three carried weapons, one a SKS rifle, the other two AK-47 automatic rifles.

At sunrise the next morning, *Rush Act* came upon a camp consisting of two hootches and four bunkers connecting the hootches. The Marines threw grenades into both hootches and bunkers, destroying all. An enemy soldier appeared, and, after a quick exchange of rifle fire, he lay dead. Two more soldiers appeared; but ran to escape the deadly Marine gunfire.

As *Rush Act's* position had now been compromised, they were extracted by helicopter and reinserted to continue patrolling at a place called Nu Da Ne.

On November 18th, Doc. Daniels, the team Corpsman, fell down a cliff, breaking his leg. The team leader immediately called for an extraction. The supporting helicopter squadron, HMM-263 launched a rescue mission. One CH-46 landed at the 1st Recon Battalion to pick up Lt. Col. Leftwich. The Colonel chose to come along to oversee the extraction. Monsoon season was well underway, and he knew the extraction would be risky; nevertheless, with one of the team seriously injured, he deemed it important to make the attempt. The weather was clearing over the team's location and they just might pull it off.

Arriving at the team's location, clouds and fog hung low over the Que Sons. It was impossible for the CH-46 to land so Lt. Col. Leftwich ordered the SPIE rig lowered. All members of the team hooked their harnesses to the rig and were successfully pulled from the jungle. Meanwhile, the clouds had closed in, obscuring some of the peaks around the helicopter. The CH-46 crashed into the mountainside. All were killed, the helicopter crew, the extraction crew (which included Lt. Col. Leftwich), and all members of the team, *Rush Act.*

Two reconnaissance teams found the crash site the next day and recovered all bodies - to be interred with full military honors.

Chapter 6 - Just Throw Rocks

In 1949, Jimmie Howard was very popular in his high school. He'd just come off a winning season in football, and earned the title of all-state tackle in the State of Iowa for the second year in a row. His team was the Greyhounds of Burlington High School. Burlington, a town on the Mississippi River in Eastern Iowa was Jimmie's home. He loved football and played it every year of high school. He also played basketball and ran track. He had, in fact, won the state track meet half-mile run, turning in a time of 2:06.2 minutes.

After high school, Jimmie went on to Iowa State University; but a year later he joined the Marines. After boot camp in San Diego, California, he managed to get on a Marine Corps football team. On a blind date he met his future wife, Theresa Maria Azevedo. She was quite impressed with him as the following description indicates:

"Jim was 6'-3". He had dark brown wavy hair and dreamy blue eyes. Very handsome, I thought."

They were married on February 17, 1951. At this time, the Marines were battling North Korean and Chinese communists on the Korean peninsula. Shortly after the birth of his first child, Jimmie Jr., Jimmie Howard received orders to go to Korea. Between August 12 and 15 of 1952, while serving as a forward observer for a mortar company, Corporal Jimmie Howard won a Silver Star. He was knocked unconscious by a mortar shell while engaged in hand-to-hand combat with the enemy; but regained consciousness and continued to fight until rendered unconscious again by another mortar shell.

It was in Vietnam, however, that Jimmie Howard would win enduring fame. When he received orders for Vietnam, his first action was to take his family to see the "Sound of Music". He was now the father of six children. His wife, Theresa, fully supported him because she had seen the evils wrought by the Chinese Communists in Shanghai, China.

In June 1966, the 1st Marine Division became concerned with the presence of NVA units in the Que Son Valley of Vietnam. To assess the strength and disposition of these enemy forces, the 1st Marine Division Commander ordered an extensive reconnaissance campaign. One of these units was an 18-man reconnaissance team, led by Staff Sergeant Jimmie Howard. They Landed on June 13, 1966 on the Nui Vu hill mass that dominates the terrain approximately 10 miles west of Tam Ky.

After their insertion on June 13th, Howard's men found the 1,500-foot hill an excellent observation post. For the next two days, they were able to call artillery fire missions on enemy movements in their area.

Unfortunately by June 15, 1966, the enemy had become wise to the patrol's presence on Hill 488. On the night of June 15, an ARVN Special Forces Camp reported an enemy

Staff Sergeant Jimmie Howard

battalion moving toward the Marine's position at Nui Vu.

SSgt Howard got his team leaders together and looked for the best spot on the hill to defend. They found a spot 5 or 6 feet from the top of the hill where they could set up a 360° perimeter in the protection of boulders and bomb craters. The group of 16 Marines and 2 Navy Corpsman then waited in the darkness for the enemy.

About 9:15 pm, the NVA attacked. Shrill whistle blasts and the clacking of bamboo sticks broke the calm of the night signaling the assault. Enemy soldiers probed the position trying to draw the Marine's fire. SSgt Howard instructed his men to hold their fire until they had a clear target. He told them "We can't afford to shoot at shadows". Each man had a rifle and four fragmentation grenades. In addition, two of the men had grenade launchers.

At 10 p.m., the NVA launched the first assault in force.

They blasted away with automatic weapons, grenades, and 60-millimeter mortars. Jimmie Howard estimated they were only 30 meters away and approaching from all sides. Next, "They opened up with four .50 caliber machine guns, one on each side of the hill", as Howard, described it. Nevertheless, the Marine held, and beat back the assault.

Twenty to twenty-five minutes later, the Communists again rushed the Marine position. Huey helicopters were now hovering overhead, but couldn't support the Marines because the pilots couldn't tell who was who on the ground. All the pilots could see were muzzle flashes and explosions. The helicopters were followed by jet fighters, but the fighter pilots couldn't tell the enemy from the friendlies. Finally a plane arrived equipped with flares. SSgt Howard got on the radio and told the crew of the flare ship where to drop the flares. With the night illuminated by flares, the Huey pilots could see the Marine position as well as the waves of enemy assaulting that position. Jimmie Howard describes that action that followed:

"The choppers came in, strafing with their machine guns and rockets, and guiding the jets in. I told 'em to drop those bombs as close to us as they could. They put 'em right in our back pockets."

The bombs landed so close that the Marines could feel heat from their explosions. Despite the fact the aircraft fired 216 rockets, 23,000 M-60 machine gun rounds, 1,750 20-mm rounds, and dropped forty-four 250-pound bombs, the enemy attacks continued. Bullets and grenade shrapnel ricocheted off the boulder spewing rock fragments among the defenders.

"We took a lot of wounds from the ricochets," Howard said.

The NVA tried to demoralize the defenders on the hill, shouting in plain English:

"Marines you die in an hour."

Howard ordered his Marines to respond by laughing at

the NVA. As the battle continued, the Marines ran out of grenades. SSgt Howard told them: "Just throw rocks."

The attackers couldn't be sure the thump they heard as a rock hit the ground, came from a rock or a grenade. When the enemy soldiers moved to avoid the potential explosion of a grenade, the Marines could target them and make their shots count.

One of Howard's men was knocked out by concussion from a grenade and the Viet Cong started to carry the Marine off; but as SSgt Howard describes:

"He came to and killed two of them with his combat knife before they killed him. When we found him in the morning, the two dead VC were lying next to him. My man still had his knife in his hand."

Another example of the tenaciousness of the defenders was the Marine who, after suffering wounds from mortar fragments and a grenade that bounced off his head and exploded, continued firing his rifle until he ran out of ammunition.

Then there was the Navy corpsman, wounded several times himself, who continued treating the wounded and fired back at the enemy as the battled ensued.

By morning, Howard had only seven men left who could still trigger a rifle. They gathered ammunition from the more seriously wounded and the dead, and redistributed it among themselves.

At 5:25 am, to buck-up his men's spirits, Jimmie Howard announced:

"OK, you people reveille goes in 35 minutes." Then he followed it up with "Reveille, Reveille" at 6am.

At sunrise a Marine reactionary company was flown to Hill 488 to relieve the embattled defenders. It took the reaction force until noon to reach Howard's perimeter on Hill 488. Five of the defenders were dead and a sixth died en route to the base camp at Chu Lai. By the time the rescue force reached SSgt Howard and his men, among the 12 survivors there remained only eight rounds of ammunition. Surrounding the hill lay 43 Viet Cong bodies; but intelligence estimated the total enemy casualties could be much higher.

Jimmie Howard suffered greatly from the attack. When operated on at Chu Lai, they removed a massive amount of shrapnel and they deep-sowed a 50-caliber bullet because of the difficulty to remove from such a delicate location.

For his action on Hill 488, Gunny Howard was awarded the Congressional Medal of Honor. President Johnson presented the medal to him in Washington, D.C., with the Gunny's wife and six children looking on. Also present at the ceremony were the other Marines, who survived that night on Hill 488.

As a further honor, the Navy named a destroyer the USS Howard. Jimmie Howard, however, was never aware of this since the Navy made the decision approximately 5 years after his death in 1993.

Chapter 7 - Dennis Storm - The Leader Everyone Loved

The CH-46 Sea Knight began its descent toward the blanket of green below. Moments before, the members of team *Lynch Law* had watched two Cobra gunships skim the tree tops below, trying to entreat any enemy present to shoot at the gunships and betray their location. If there were Gooks down there, they didn't take the bait, because the insert bird was going in.

Lt. Dennis Storm, Commanding Officer of Bravo Company, was the Insert Officer that day. He walked to the rear ramp of the helicopter and peered out. He gave the signal to the crew to lower the ramp. The seven men of the recon team waited for the swaying of the helicopter to cease, signaling its gear had contacted the ground of the landing zone (LZ). To their surprise, the helicopter continued to hover; but a mass of waving grass appeared outside the back ramp. Lt. Storm signaled for the team to exit the chopper. The team was being inserted on a knoll with insufficient area for the pilot to set the helicopter down.

The first two team members stepped off the ramp. Then it happened. The helicopter lurched upward, rising a hundred feet or so in a matter of seconds. The remaining members of the team dropped back into their seats. Lt Storm, being in the middle aisle, fell to the deck of the helicopter. There was nothing for the lieutenant to grasp and the nose of the aircraft tilted upward with the result that he went sliding toward the lowered ramp. Not wanting to lose their favorite officer, every man of team *Lynch Law* lunged to grasp him. Not a moment too late. Lt. Storm didn't stop sliding until half his body was off the ramp, legs dangling in the air. The Marines pulled him back in and helped him to his feet. The helicopter descended again and the other team members successfully inserted. The bond between Lt. Storm and the team probably could be credited for saving his life, for even a moment's hesitation on the part of the team would have had fatal consequences.

Dennis Storm chose the Marine Corps as his career. As an Officer of Marines he could use his rank to command respect and obedience of his men. He could have also been like many "hard-core" Marines – shouted and threatened punishment to motivate his troops. Neither of these were Lt. Storm's style. He had his own special charisma. He was able to get the best from his men because he cared about them, and they knew he cared.

Recon wasn't Lt. Storm's first assignment, however. Arriving in Vietnam in January 1969, he was first assigned as a platoon commander with "G" Company, 2nd Battalion, 5th Marine Regiment. He led his platoon on operations Taylor Common I and II, Durham Peak, Muskegee Meadows and Forsyth Graves. On March 28, 1969, Lt. Storm was wounded while leading his men on an operation in a particularly hostile area of Vietnam known as "Arizona Territory".

Back in the Arizona Territory again, on May 10, 1969, Lt. Storm's company got in a firefight, which resulted in the company commander being wounded. When the commander was evacuated, Lt. Storm took command of the company. He reorganized the troops and fought the Communist troops through the night and into the next day. After a night of relentless assault by the Marines, the enemy broke and ran, leaving behind a 75 mm recoilless rifle – a weapon of great value to the Vietnamese insurgents.

On May 15, 1969, his troops got into it with the enemy again. This time they ran into a large force of the North Vietnamese Army. The NVA poured a heavy volume of small arms fire at the Marines from well-entrenched emplacements on both sides of the Marines.

Lt. Storm led his men in an assault on the enemy positions. Then, realizing the tactic risked heavy Marine casualties, he ordered his men to withdraw to a more easily defended position. Receiving artillery support, the rest of Lt. Storm's company withdrew to allow the big guns to work over the enemy without endangering the Marines.

Unfortunately one of Lt. Storm's squads was cut off and pinned down by the NVA. Dennis immediately went to their aid. He mustered a small group of Marines and led them through the bullet-riddled terrain to the trapped squad. He managed to identify the main source of North Vietnamese fire. Concentrating on this source, he led the squad and relief troops in an assault on the enemy position. Causing the NVA to back off momentarily, the whole group of Marines maneuvered back to friendly lines.

The NVA counter attacked and attempted to overrun the Marine platoons. Dennis Storm moved among his men's positions, disregarding the incoming enemy round, to direct the Marines fire and encouraged them. The Marine riflemen fired so deadly and accurately, that the North Vietnamese

Army were forced back into the artillery barrage.

Soon helicopter gunships and fixed-wing aircraft arrived to assist the Marines on the ground. Lt. Storm seized the opportunity and moved forward of his defense perimeter and marked the enemy positions with smoke grenades to assist the aircraft in locating targets. Then, when helicopters arrived to resupply the Marines on the ground, he exposed himself to enemy fire. He stood up to guide the supply helicopters to the landing zone with a flashlight. For his actions during this fight, Lt. Dennis Storm was awarded the Silver Star Medal.

In August of 1969, Dennis Storm was assigned to the Battalion Staff of the 2nd Battalion, 5th Marines. Was this to be an end to his exploits in the bush? – Not hardly. On November 17, 1969, while accompanying the Battalion Command Group on another operation in "Arizona Territory," he captured two NVA trying to escape across the Son Vu Gia River.

Then on December 7, 1969, while occupying the Battalion's command post in Quang Nam Province, he saw a helicopter crash near the battalion landing zone. Running to the burning aircraft, he helped the shocked and injured passengers to safety. He discovered the crew chief wasn't among the others escaping the burning aircraft. Despite the fire and exploding ammunition. Lt. Storm ran aboard the flaming wreckage through the rear section. He located the crew chief near the forward portion of the helicopter under several pieces of heavy debris. He summoned two other Marines and the three of them were able to extract the crew chief from the wreckage and get him to an area where the crew chief's wounds could be treated. For his actions on December 7th, Lt. Storm was awarded the Navy and Marine Corps Medal.

In January 1970, Lt. Dennis M. Storm transferred to the 1st Reconnaissance Battalion. On March 3, 1970, Colonel

Lieutenant Storm

Drumright, Commander of the 1st Reconnaissance Battalion, assigned him to be the Commanding Officer of Company "B", more commonly called "Bravo" company.

The following months were rough on the 1st Reconnaissance Battalion and Bravo Company in particular. In March 1970, with antiwar protest growing stronger every day in the United States, President Nixon was anxious to speed up troop withdrawals. Withdrawing the Marine units, which had been in active combat against the VC/NVA left something of a void.

To compensate, 1ˢᵗ Recon Battalion was ordered to increase the number of patrols and, more often, to call artillery fire missions or air strikes on enemy positions they discovered in the field. For Recon this meant more patrols in the bush and greater chance of having to fight their way out of contact with the enemy. Non-combat losses took their toll also, with accidents and malaria being two of the main culprits.

As a result, Bravo Company, by June 1970 was considerably under strength with most of the Marines pulling double duty. At the same time, the company 1st Sergeant seemed to have a heart of stone, not appearing to care about the extra burden being placed on the Marines of the Company.

Lt. Storm, however, could motivate even the grouchiest Marine in his command. For instance, when the lieutenant walked through the company area, it was not uncommon for him to pause for a question and then get to talking to the Marines on a person-to-person basis. He even did this returning from the showers to his company quarters. In these conversations he would encourage his men saying things like: "The way to get along with the 1ˢᵗ Sgt is to call him by his 1ˢᵗ name – God." Lt. Storm also pointed out that virtually every President of the United States had done military service and this period his Marines were currently struggling through might just be the beginning of a much more prominent career. In addition, the lieutenant entertained his men with stories of his more amusing of his exploits in the bush. One of these being the time he found himself alone when the insert helicopters were departing.

Lt. Storm went on reconnaissance patrols also. On May 11, 1970 he was inserted as leader of a team with the call sign *Policy Game*. For two days *Policy Game* patrolled across steep terrain, with vines, bamboo, elephant grass, boulders, thorns, thick bushes, and deadfall (dead branches from the trees and bushes). The patrol could only manage to make about 50 meters per hour, and couldn't avoid making noise because there was so much deadfall.

About 2:30 on the afternoon of May 13, 1970, the last man on the team, dubbed "Tail-end Charlie", heard movement in the brush to their rear. Coming up on the team from behind were three of the enemy. Two were wearing black pajamas, the usual outfit worn by the Viet Cong and the third wore a khaki uniform – more commonly the uniform of the NVA. The team got into a firefight with the three, killing one, and possibly killing the second; but then the team started receiving fire from the north. Next they heard movement to their south. Lt. Storm requested an Air Observer. When the Air Observer arrived, he directed *Policy Game* to a site where they could be extracted by ladder.

Arriving at the landing zone, the team spotted enemy movement to their northeast. They reported the location to the air observer who flew several runs against that position, laying down machine gun fire. Shortly after, helicopter gunships came on station. Spotting the same enemy activity to the team's northeast, the gunships assaulted that position with rockets, mini-guns and grenades. While this was happening, the team climbed the ladder and hooked on. Once on the ladder, the enemy fired on them from the south, southeast, north, and west. The team fired back and between them and supporting artillery battery the Marines killed two more of the enemy.

Dennis Storm survived Vietnam to continue his career in the Marine Corps and raise a family. Although he was decorated for his bravery during his service in Vietnam; perhaps his greatest contribution was the example he set for his men.

Chapter 8 - Man Vs. Tiger

A Marine serving in Vietnam faced many hazards. Beyond the enemy forces, there were the natural hazards of the jungle. While some of the smaller hazards, like snakes were potentially more deadly, running into a 400-pound tiger, a clearly visible predator was likely more hair-raising.

The problem of tigers is particularly interesting. Of course tigers were native to Vietnam, so seeing one would not be particularly unusual. Most wild animals have an instinctive fear of man. However, armed conflict of one kind or another had existed in Vietnam since the outbreak of World War II, and tigers were no longer afraid of the sounds of gunfire. In fact, they had "learned" that gunfire meant dead bodies – potentially a meal they wouldn't have to chase.

Wildlife biologists identified the tiger species living in Vietnam as the Indo-Chinese tiger. Their favorite prey consists of various species of deer and wild pigs. They will, however, attack young elephants and take smaller animals like monkeys, birds, reptiles and fish. The tiger eats 40 – 70 pounds of meat at a time. A large prey will feed the tiger for about a week if other animals don't feed on it. Tigers prefer to hunt between dusk and dawn. They usually attack from the rear, first stalking it, then striking with a rush and a leap. The tiger's main target is the neck. The tiger usually holds on to the neck until the animal dies of suffocation. This method of killing minimizes the prey's ability to fight back.

Wildlife biologists generally attribute a tiger becoming a "man-eating" tiger to man encroaching on the tiger's habitat. During the Vietnam War, the tiger's habitat was reduced by bombing, artillery strikes and defoliation by spraying parts of the jungle with chemicals that kill the leaves of plants. In addition, an area which provided a good hiding place for the enemy, was also likely to be ideal tiger habitat. Since Recon Marines had to patrol these areas, it was only natural the Marines would eventually encounter a tiger.

At about 7:00 p.m. on December 22, 1968, team *Barrister*, from the 3rd Reconnaissance Battalion began to settle into their harbor site. The team had been on patrol since noon on December 20, and was looking forward to being extracted back to the Battalion encampment and hot chow. The area where they'd been patrolling had steep hills, heavy underbrush, and elephant grass. Patrolling this area was exhausting. Encounters with the enemy had been at a distance.

The first encounter was the sound of enemy movement to their west and north. They called for an artillery fire mission; but were unable to assess the effect, except that the movement ceased. The next day, December 21, the team spotted what appeared to be an enemy entrenchment. They called for an air strike.

The support aircraft dropped napalm on the enemy position. Secondary explosions occurred as the napalm burned, signaling the enemy had some type of ammunition stored at the site. Later that day the team spotted two VC/NVA sitting on top of a hill. The team called a fire mission and air strike on this position. A scream from the target area indicated the strike had at least been partially successful.

On December 22, the team heard movement around them throughout the day. *Barrister* responded by calling for artillery and air support on two occasions; but had no idea how effective these were. Finally the team settled in the harbor site, awaiting the extract helicopters. Bad weather signaled that they might have to spend another night in the bush. Two men took the first watch as the others settled down to sleep.

A scream pierced the relative silence of the jungle. Someone else yelled, "It's a tiger! It's a tiger!"

PFC Roy Regan woke to find a tiger holding Sgt. Goolden in his mouth. PFC Thomas E. Shainline instinctively jumped at the tiger in the hope the animal would release the sergeant. The tiger tried to escape with his prey, dragging the sergeant to a bomb crater 10 meters away. The team responded, following the tiger to the bomb crater, firing at the beast until he released Sgt. Goolden. As the sergeant staggered from the bomb crater, the team ensured the cat was dead.

The sergeant's first words were, "What happened?"

The team administered first aid to the sergeant. Not long after, a CH-46 helicopter arrived, picked up the team and the dead tiger. Sgt. Goolden was rushed to the 3rd Medical Battalion Hospital at Quang Tri. Here the medical personnel treated the lacerations and bites on Sgt. Goolden's neck, inflicted by the tiger. The tiger, nine feet long from head to tail was dropped off with the team at 3rd Reconnaissance Battalion. The 400 - pound beast was strung up on a ten-foot scaffold to be examined by the team, and other members of the Battalion.

Major General Raymond G. Davis, Commanding General, 3rd Marine Division and his Assistant Division Commander, Brigadier General Robert B. Carney, Jr., also examined the tiger and congratulated the team for killing the animal.

In addition, a professional Vietnamese tiger hunter named Sang observed the hanging tiger. Mr. Sang had organized a tiger hunt in response to the killing of a Marine by a tiger six weeks earlier. Mr. Sang told the Marines he had killed five tigers in his 20 years of hunting; but had never seen one as large as this one. Due to the wounds inflicted by the tiger, Sgt. Goodlen was medically retired from the Marine Corps.

Another victim of the Indo-Chinese tiger was Sergeant Robert Crain Phleger. Presumably the tigers have no preference for rank and the fact that one attacked Sgt. Phleger was only coincidence. Sgt. Phleger was a member of 1st Force Reconnaissance Company. His first assignment with the company was as a radio repair technician.

Phleger stood 5 foot 10 inches tall, wore dark-horned rimmed glasses, and wore his hair very shortly cropped in the fashion of most Recon Marines. He was partial to a bit of snuff, making a ritual of dipping a bit. He was very approachable and cheerful and openly demonstrated his concern for the junior Marines of his communications platoon. As a sole surviving son, Sgt. Phelger was legally exempt from combat duty; yet he signed a waiver, which allowed him to serve in Vietnam. In addition, he petitioned Lt. Holly, Operations Officer, to allow him to participate in long-range reconnaissance patrols. He progressed from primary radio operator to assistant team leader, then, he was assigned to be the leader of team *Rock Mat*.

On May 5, 1970, as team *Rock Mat* rode in the truck taking them to an airstrip to board their aircraft, Corporal Smith teased Sgt. Phleger about the sergeant's recent

Marriage and how Corporal Smith would have to take over the team because the bush was no place for an "old married man".

The team was inserted at a place called Razorback Ridge. From time of insertion, *Rock Mat* climbed to high ground to find a good location for communications and observation. About 6:00 p.m. the team stopped to eat chow then sought out a harbor site. The Razorback was too narrow and rocky to allow the team to assume the usual 360-degree circle for the night. Instead, they were strung out, single file, with Sgt. Phleger at one end of the line. Communications with the rear were poor and the Marines in the rear couldn't be sure if whomever was on radio watch was awake.

About 10:00 p.m., the Marines not yet asleep heard rustling in the bush and what sounded like muffled screams from Sgt. Phleger. They radioed to the rear that it sounded like their team leader was fighting someone in the bush. Then all they heard was silence. Lt. Holly radioed back to the team to stay calm and alert, suggesting the Sgt. may have had a nightmare and wandered off in his sleep.

The team members, however, worried the NVA had come upon Sgt. Phleger and, after a struggle, taken him prisoner. They thought about searching for him in the dark. Using their flashlights would make the task easier, but would give their position away. The team felt around in the dark for a while, always concerned that anyone of them might be the next to disappear if NVA forces had indeed discovered their position. After a time, failing to locate their team leader, Corporal Smith took over the team and radioed their situation back to Operations. All the members of the team stayed awake the rest of the night, weapons ready for whatever foe lurked in the darkness.

When dawn finally broke, the team located the spot where Sgt. Phleger had bedded down for the night. There lay his rifle, pack, gas mask, and cartridge belt. The NVA would not likely have left the rifle and cartridge belt. An aura of mystery prevailed. As the team searched further, they found the sergeant's hat and poncho liner, both covered in blood. They radioed back to tell Operations what they found and that they also could see drag marks leading from the site. Operations told them to follow the drag marks.

Following the drag marks, first the team spotted Sgt. Phleger's boots sticking out from alongside a bush. Corporal Smith radioed back they had found Phleger. As Smith transmitted this radio message, a huge roar from a tiger not more than 15 feet away shocked the team. The team fired their rifles at the tiger; but it disappeared into the bush. The team turned to examine the body only to find the tiger had consumed most of the corpse from the waist up.

The team prepared for extract with the remains of Sgt. Phleger. They were confident they had scared the man-eating tiger off when they fired their weapons at it. Another tremendous roar informed them the tiger had returned to claim the rest of his kill. Again, the team fired at the vicious cat and even threw a grenade at it as it darted off into the bush.

When the extract helicopter finally arrived, the team carried the body of Sgt. Phleger, wrapped in a poncho, aboard the aircraft. The body was later autopsied. From the autopsy, it was determined that the sergeant had been asleep with his poncho over his head when the tiger attacked. The tiger apparently killed his victim by breaking his neck. None of team *Rock Mat* ever returned to the bush.

On May 17th, team *Wage Earner*, from Echo Company, 1st Reconnaissance Battalion, had just completed an uneventful three-day patrol. The area they had been assigned to patrol had steep slopes with a canopy formed by trees 60 feet above them and very dense undergrowth consisting of vines, small bushes, bamboo, grass, and thorn bushes. The team found movement very difficult, being able to only move about 100 meters an hour. The team also observed signs of elephants as well as boars and squirrels. This area was near a place the Marines called Elephant Valley.

When the extract helicopter arrived, Sgt. Larkins, the assistant team leader, positioned himself to count team members as they boarded the CH-46 to make sure no one was left behind. Inside the helicopter, other team members saw a blur of movement in the bush behind the sergeant. They signaled frantically to him.

When he turned around he saw large tiger charging straight for him. The sergeant dropped to the kneeling firing position, took careful aim at the orange and white head, and squeezed off a round. This first round deflected the tiger sufficiently from his direction of attack to allow Sgt. Larkins to empty the rest of his magazine of rounds into the tiger. The tiger finally dropped dead less than fifteen feet from where Sgt. Larkins stood.

When the team arrived at the 1st Reconnaissance Battalion LZ. Sgt. Larkins and the team leader, Lt. Daugherty, hauled the trophy tiger off the helicopter with the tiger lashed to the pole they bore. Sgt. Larkins coolness facing the charging tiger made him something of a legend among the other men of 1st Reconnaissance Battalion, especially since his last rifle qualification scores barely qualified him as a marksman.

Tiger Bagged by Sgt. Larkins

Chapter 9 - "Wild Bill Drumright"

William Drumright never did anything half-heartedly. Schoolmates from Cohn High School in Nashville, Tennessee can vouch for that.

Bill's parents moved to Nashville in 1929. In 1942 Bill started school at Cohn High School. The school was located across the street from the four-block long city park. The park was a favorite hangout for Bill and his friends. There they would play softball, basketball, tennis or just enjoy lying on the grass under the shade trees talking.

Bill liked football best, and played both guard and defensive end on the high school team for three years. He was a tough blocker and tackler; but his most memorable moment at Cohn was in the game against West End High school. West End was Cohn's greatest rival. At one point in the game, West End had driven the football down to within the 5-yard line of Cohn and threatened to score. As two of the Cohn players tackled the West End ball carrier, the ball popped out of his hands and into those of Bill Drumright.

Bill was off in a flash – dashing 99 yards for a touchdown – out running all pursuers. The Cohn Tigers went on to close out the season with 10 victories and no defeats.

Bill's performance on the football field won him an athletic scholarship to Tennessee Tech at Cookeville, Tennessee. At Tech, Bill Drumright played football for an additional four years. As teammate Joe Lancaster describes: "He played football with real gusto. As a blocker he threw himself at an opposing player anyway it took to bring him down." Bill was popular off the field also, he was a member of the "T" club and Health and Physical Education Club. He was elected Vice-President of the "T" club and also President of his Junior Class.

In the summer of 1950, North Korea invaded South Korea and started the Korean War. When the football team at Tennessee Tech reported for fall practice, the coach, worried that he would start losing team members to the military services, took the team to the Tennessee National Guard recruiter and tried to convince them to join. As National Guardsmen they would be able to perform service in Tennessee, continue at college, and avoid being shipped to Korea.

Bill didn't join the Guard. He did play football that fall and graduated the following spring with a Bachelor of Science in Health and Physical Education. Immediately after graduating from college, Bill enlisted in the Marines. Being a college graduate, he qualified for, and was soon off to Officers Candidate School. He was an honor candidate from OCS. In February of 1952, now a lieutenant in the Marine Corps, Drumright sailed to Korea for service with the 1st Marine Division. There he spent thirteen months as a rifle platoon commander, earning a Navy Commendation Medal, a Purple

Drumright the Football Player

Heart, and the Silver Star.

    After Korea, William Drumright was assigned to Yorktown, Virginia, then he returned to the southern Midwest to serve as a procurement officer. His next assignment was as a Tactics Instructor at the Basic Officers School in Quantico, Virginia. He spent three years at this assignment. In 1962 he returned to Korea where he was assigned as General Staff Advisor for the Republic of Korea Marine Corps (ROK Division located at Pohang, Korea. After this assignment in Korea, Bill Drumright returned to Nashville, Tennessee where taught in the Naval ROTC unit at Vanderbilt University. For three years at Vanderbilt he provided guidance for the three hundred Midshipman Battalion destined to become Navy and

Drumright – Marine Officer

Marine Officers.

Following the Vanderbilt assignment and a promotion to Lieutenant Colonel, William Drumright was assigned as Commanding Officer of the Second Reconnaissance Battalion, Second Marine Division, Camp LeJeune, North Carolina. Here Lt. Col. Drumright learned the techniques employed by recon Marines. He attended jungle operations in the Panama Canal Zone, submarine operations in San Juan, Puerto Rico and amphibious reconnaissance training at Camp LeJeune.

From the 2nd Recon Battalion, Lt. Col. Drumright went to the Mediterranean for eight months. Here he served as Commanding Officer, Battalion Landing Team (BLT) 1st Battalion, 2nd Marine Regiment. One of the highlights of this assignment was having the French Foreign Legion act as aggressors during a practice amphibious landing. Col. Drumright said they were the most disciplined soldiers he had seen.

In July 1969, Lt. Col. Drumright took command of Battalion Landing Team, 2nd Battalion, 26th Marine Regiment in Vietnam. His unit was assigned an area of operations (AO), which extended from north of Da Nang to North of the Ha Van Mountains, a distance of 40 miles.

In January 1970, Col. Drumright received what might have been his most challenging assignment. Major General Edwin B. Wheeler, Commander of the 1st Marine Division, asked Lt. Colonel Drumright to take command of the 1st Reconnaissance Battalion.

Due to the growing unpopularity of the Vietnam War back in the United States, President Nixon felt pressured to demonstrate that he would end the involvement of American troops in Vietnam. To do this, he ordered his commanders to plan an orderly withdrawal of the troops from Vietnam. This objective of this plan was to gradually turn over the responsibility for fighting the communists to the South Vietnamese military. The plan was called Vietnamization.

This plan, in turn, put a lot of pressure on General Wheeler. The 3rd Marine Division Forces had already left Vietnam. They had been operating in the most Northern parts of Vietnam, along the DMZ and the border with Laos. With the 3rd Marine Division gone, NVA infiltration into South Vietnam increased. General Wheeler knew there were four to five divisions of NVA operating in the area of responsibility assigned to the 1st Marine Division.

The Marine infantry units, (commonly called "grunts") now had primarily defensive responsibilities. They were deployed in the lowland areas with the mission of defending heavily populated areas against infiltration by NVA and VC. Thus, the main combat units General Wheeler commanded were spread thin and more vulnerable to enemy rocket and mortar attacks. On top of that, even these forces were scheduled for eventual withdrawal, with the Marines becoming more dependent the ability of the Army of the

Republic of Vietnam (ARVN) to shoulder the brunt of the war.

General Wheeler wanted some means of keeping the Communist forces on the defensive as the troop withdrawal progressed. He decided to rely on the Stingray concept. The 3rd Marine Division used this concept with great success in their area of responsibility. It consisted of saturating the enemy base areas with small, well-armed patrols, who were supported by artillery and combat aircraft. These patrols sought out enemy base camps and supply dumps. When they discovered these they could call for an air strike or artillery fire mission to destroy the enemy target. Occasionally they would also ambush smaller enemy units. Often they would locate the coordinates of the enemy positions for later assault by bombers, artillery or large-scale infantry units. In this way the Marines kept pressure on the VC and NVA, seriously impeding the enemy's ability to mount offensives.

General Wheeler needed troops trained to conduct small-scale patrols in mountainous and heavily forested terrain, which the enemy used as refuge. He decided to assign the task to the 1st Reconnaissance Battalion. To successfully employ the Stingray concept, required a special leader.

General Wheeler wanted a man who was aggressive, courageous, but with charisma. He chose Colonel William Drumright, Commander of the 2nd Battalion, 26th Marine Regiment. By this time Lt. Col. Drumright's reputation merited the nickname, "Wild Bill". General Wheeler called Colonel Drumright to Division Headquarters and asked him to take the assignment. Drumright accepted; but agreed only on certain conditions. He addressed the General:

"General, I can do what you want. I can make 'em fight. But I am goin' to need lots of support, and I mean dedicated assets ... All day, every day, twenty-four hours a day. My boys has got to know that if'n they get in the ----, we are gonna get them out!" [5]

Col. Drumright also insisted on his authority to choose

lieutenants to lead his troops:

"I want authority to hire, fire and recruit – no questions asked. I want my pick from Two-twenty-six first, then wherever else we find 'em." [5]

The reason Drumright insisted on choosing his own lieutenants was that he wanted the best to lead his men. He wanted men who had already proven themselves in combat. He also knew that Marine lieutenants had very extensive training in small unit tactics, scouting and patrolling, land navigation, and the use of supporting arms. Drumright also wanted the authority to replace any lieutenant that couldn't meet the challenge of the new mission.

William Drumright took over the 40 odd officers and six hundred enlisted men of the 1st Reconnaissance Battalion on January 27, 1970. Wheeler wanted Drumright to keep not less than thirty teams in the field at all times. In addition, 1st Recon was given the responsibility of providing security for four fortified observation posts (OP's) overlooking the major avenues of approach into the population centers included in the 1st Marine Division's area of responsibility.

One of Col. Drumright's first actions was to screen the records of the lieutenants assigned to the battalion looking for any that hadn't been in the bush for an extended period of time. He found ten and sent them to Division Headquarters for reassignment. These men he replaced by some of his own choosing from 2/26 and elsewhere in the division. Next he roused the troops, the staff non-commissioned officers, and other officers into a state of anxiety. He wanted his Marines to be more afraid of him than the enemy and their leaders to care for their men.

Colonel Drumright also insisted his staff provide the best conditions they could for the troops when they were in the rear at Camp Reasoner. The mess hall served the best food in the division – a welcome treat for a team who came back after five to seven days in the bush.

Colonel Drumright thought the world of his reconnaissance Marines. He firmly believed that it was the young enlisted Marine who refused to yield his piece of ground to the enemy that meant the difference between victory and defeat. When new Marines arrived in the battalion, they had to attend an 11-day reconnaissance indoctrination program (RIP). This was a refresher course that was specially adapted to prepare these Marines for situations unique to Vietnam.

Col. Drumright would greet the men on the first day of the program as they were assembled in the open-air amphitheater, which also served as a movie theater and stage for USO shows. He would tell the men what he expected of them; but would inspire them with a few tales of his own exploits in the bush. When a team made contact with the enemy in the bush and had to be extracted, Col. Drumright rode the emergency extract helicopter armed with a rifle to help provide covering fire during the extraction. When the extracted team returned to the LZ at 1st Recon Battalion, Drumright would shake each man's hand in appreciation for his performance.

When Colonel Drumright left 1st Recon in August 1970, the battalion itself was being down sized. By the end of September 1970, only Alpha and Bravo companies were left to continue the reconnaissance mission. Colonel Drumright continued to serve the Marine Corps throughout the 1970's and into the 1980's. He used his experience in combat and particularly with reconnaissance Marines to guide staff at Headquarters Marine Corps in planning for the training and equipping Marines for future combat. Nevertheless William Drumright was a warrior and the champion of all who took up arms in the defense of the United States, its people, and its allies. Nothing was more important to Colonel Drumright than his "boys". After his retirement, he would hold reunions at his home in Tennessee, extending his hospitality to those whom he had served with and commanded in the past.

[5] *Reluctant Warrior,* pages 317-318.

Chapter 10 - Team *Box Score*

Private First Class Michael P. Nation watched as five VC/NCA moved along a ridgeline approximately 700 meters away. He was one of the eight men who composed the recon team *Box Score*. The others included team leader Second Lieutenant Terry Graves, Corpsman Steve Thompson, Corporal Danny Slocum, Corporal Robert Thompson, Lance Corporal Steven Emrick, PFC Adrian Lopez, and PFC James Honeycutt. This team was truly representative of the United States. Each of them came from a different region of the country.

It was February 16, 1968 and Lieutenant Graves had only been with *Box Score* for a short time, having made his first patrol in mid-January 1968. Terrence C. Graves came from Groton, New York. He attended school at Edmeston Central School in Edmeston, New York. An avid sports enthusiast, he went out for football, basketball, and baseball. He excelled at baseball, but he was also a serious student, driving himself to achieve the position of salutorian of his

Kit Carson Scout UNK — Cpl. Danny M. Slocum — 2ndLt. Terry Graves
Ray Warren — Sgt. William H. Andress — Pfc. Mike Nations

10 January 1968
John Kaulu — HM3 Steve Thompson — Cpl. Robert B. Thompson

Team Boxscore

class. At Edmeston he had a friendly rivalry with a classmate, Barbara Finley, in the academic arena. He never managed to "best" her; but respected her abilities. Terry was a leader at Edmeston.

As Barbara describes: "He always knew what to say and how to say it." She also said Terry had "looks, intelligence, charisma, confidence, manners and a great sense of humor. His smile lit up a room."

His skill at baseball won him a position on the Doubleday team at Cooperstown, Ohio. His performance with that team, in turn, attracted the attention of the Cincinnati Reds who asked him to try out for their team.

The offer came, however, right at the time when Terry had prepared to enter the University of Miami at Ohio. Terry chose college instead. At Miami he entered ROTC and achieved the rank of Battalion Commander his senior year there. Upon graduation he headed for Quantico, and soon won his commission as a Second Lieutenant in the United States Marine Corps.

Now as the leader of a team of recon Marines, he had deployed his men in their usual 360-degree defensive positions in a bomb crater. His hope was for a successful prisoner snatch. Since his Marine superiors had determined prisoners were the most valuable source of intelligence information, Terry hope to take a prisoner or prisoners. This would also mean the team would be extracted immediately, allowing them to return to the relative comfort of their base. On his first patrol back in January after a successful prisoner snatch, Terry's team was treated to a steak dinner and three days of rest and relaxation (R&R) at Da Nang. Terry hoped to give his team this privilege again.

Lt. Graves saw PFC Nation motion him to look at the enemy movement. Now instead of five, seven enemy soldiers were visible. Lieutenant Graves led Danny Slocum, Lopez, and Robert B. Thompson up on the ridgeline along the trail to ambush them. When the VC were five meters from PFC Nation, the Lieutenant, Lopez and Thompson, the five of them opened up on the enemy. Doc Thompson and LCpl. Emerick held their fire as they were on the other side of the trail.

All seven of the enemy soldiers were killed. Unfortunately the enemy managed to get off a few rounds, two of which hit Danny Slocum, tearing away shin and muscle from his thigh; but not producing life-threatening wounds. The team stopped firing and listened for any sounds of additional enemy movement. Hearing nothing, they went to search the bodies for any papers, which might be of intelligence value. They did find a diary and a pack, which they decided might have some value.

Lt. Graves ordered the team to withdraw to a small hill, a location he felt suitable for an emergency medical evacuation of the wounded Slocum and team *Box Score* whose position had now been compromised by the firefight. As the team attempted to withdraw to this position, they were raked by rounds from enemy automatic weapons from two different positions. Graves ordered his team into their defensive positions and they began to return fire. Corporal Thompson, using his M-79 grenade launcher, managed to knock out several enemy positions. Cpl. Thompson was assisted in this task by PFC Nation, who exposed himself to enemy fire, firing tracers at the enemy positions. The tracers helped Thompson aim the M-79 and accurately place the grenades.

Cpl. Thompson's grenade attack brought a short lull in the battle. Nonetheless, the gunfire had attracted at least two companies of NVA who were now attempting to surround the eight-man patrol. Lt. Graves knew they couldn't be extracted from their current position and needed to move to a better one. Compounding the problem was the fact that Slocum was injured and couldn't walk without assistance. As they tried to move Slocum, enemy rounds impacted around them. They had to put Slocum down again. Thompson, Honeycutt and Emrick moved on up to the top of the hill. Lt. Graves called for air strikes.

A CH-46 attempted to land on the hill; but was driven off by automatic weapons fire. Then Lt. Graves suffered a wound to his thigh. Doc Thompson moved to tend to the Lieutenant's wound. In the meanwhile, Emrick, operating a radio, continued to direct supporting artillery and airstrikes from the hilltop. As Doc Thompson began to apply a dressing to Lieutenant Grave's wound, Corporal Thompson got hit. He was wounded in the lower abdomen. In fact, the bullet had gone through the abdominal cavity and fractured his pelvic bones as well.

As Doc Thompson began to work on Cpl. Thompson, the Corporal passed out. Doc tried to revive his teammate with cardiopulmonary resuscitation. While he was engaged in doing this, Lopez called out to the Corpsman that Emrick had been hit.

Doc had his hands full trying to revive Thompson, so he yelled for PFC Nation to do what he could for Emrick.

Emrick repeatedly pleaded, "Get the radio off." Lopez managed to remove the radio by snapping off the bottom of the pack. Then Emrick said, "Oh my God," and passed out. Nation gave him mouth-to-mouth respiration in an attempt to revive him. Danny Slocum took over the radio and reported their situation to the Command Post, describing the injuries and requesting assistance. All this time, the enemy kept firing on the Marines. Marine aircraft continued to bomb the area around them.

Lieutenant Graves told his men, "We still have to get to the south side of the knoll." Doc Thompson and Honeycutt dragged Corporal Thompson and Nation and Lopez dragged Emrick up the hill. Graves and Slocum provided covering gunfire as the group struggled to the top of the ridgeline.

The ridgeline was a good location for a helicopter extraction; but, unfortunately, had higher hills on either side of it. NVA occupied these hills and could raise havoc with any attempt to rescue team *Box Score*. A second CH-46 came in to rescue the team. It took heavy fire and had to regain altitude. Next Captain David Underwood, pilot of a H-34 helicopter decided to try for the extraction. He followed a Huey gunship, which provided suppressing fire. They came in at treetop level and were met by a hail of enemy gunfire. Captain Underwood managed to set his bird down only a few meters from the team. Enemy rounds tore out the side windows, and ripped up the instrument panel. Then the fuselage and fuel pods were hit. Underwood spotted the team and held the bird steady, to give them an opportunity to reach him.

The team came on, dragging the wounded and stopping periodically to fire back at their attackers. Due to the intense fire, Captain Underwood decided not to risk calling in another helicopter to assist with the extraction. Instead, he ordered the whole team to board his aircraft. Honeycutt and Lopez helped Emrick and Nation board the helicopter. Lieutenant Graves, rifle in one hand and, radio mike in another, moved to the helicopter, firing at the enemy and talking into the mike. Another burst of enemy automatic fire sent aircraft fuel spraying all over. The helicopter was now severely damaged and Captain Underwood was finding it difficult to control. Lt. Graves, seeing the extent of damage to the helicopter yelled at the pilot to "Get out" and waved him off.

Captain Underwood didn't see the Lieutenant; but, thinking all the team was on board, took off. As Underwood took off, the NVA swarmed toward the chopper to get better shots. One bullet hit Lopez, who was now aboard the helicopter, striking first his thigh and then burrowing into his stomach. The helicopter was a few feet off the ground when Slocum and Honeycutt realized Lt. Graves had been left behind to deal with the enemy alone. Both jumped from the helicopter to assist the lieutenant. With this reduction in weight, Captain Underwood was able to gain altitude quickly and make a successful flight to the nearest medical facility in the crippled bird.

Back at the firefight, another H-34 pilot, Captain Bergman, decided to try for the three-team members left behind. Again, following a Huey gunship, the helicopter pair made three unsuccessful passes before they located the remnants of team *Box Score*. When Captain Bergman first set down his crew chief was badly wounded so he had to fly to the nearest medical facility. He unloaded the wounded crew chief, then discovered his helicopter was leaking fuel so he was unable to return to the beleaguered team members.

A Huey helicopter made the next attempt to rescue Graves, Slocum, and Honeycutt. The pilot radioed to the team to move further south where the gunfire was less intense. The team members managed to comply. When the Huey came in, it hovered about a foot off the ground. The team members got to the bird and threw their packs in, then climbed in. When the helicopter got about five feet above the ground, enemy rounds tore through the back of the helicopter, hitting the co-pilot and apparently wounding the pilot, because, as Slocum describes: (the chopper) "...went spastic."

The helicopter then landed on its side, Slocum ending on top of a pile of bodies.

Slocum pulled himself out and saw one of the pilots lying on the ground. The pilot was still alive. Seeing about fifteen to twenty enemy soldiers approaching, Slocum asked the pilot if he had a pistol. The pilot said no but that there was a rifle inside the cabin. Slocum climbed in the cabin for the rifle only to find the enemy was now only five to six meters away. They fired at him, rounds impacting on either side of him. Slocum dashed for the cover of a nearby streambed.

There he managed to find enough cover to hide himself from his pursuers. During the night he heard more helicopters approach, followed by he sounds of a firefight. Unknown to Slocum at the time, a reaction force of infantrymen from Bravo Company, 1st Battalion, 4th Marine Regiment had been brought in to search for survivors at the site of the crashed helicopter. The reaction team encountered fire from three sides as they approached the helicopter, and were forced to withdraw to defensible positions.

The next morning the rest of Bravo Company arrived and made it to the helicopter. They found that Graves and Honeycutt had been killed, with Slocum missing in action. Slocum attempted to approach the infantrymen. When the grunts saw Slocum, they mistook him for the enemy and called an artillery fire mission on him. Slocum found a hole and lay in it as 5 or 6 artillery shells impacted around him. After this the grunts approached him. Slocum first thought them to be NVA and backed off, but a helicopter spotted him and helped him join up with infantrymen without being fired on again. Slocum was then medevaced to Cam Rahn Bay

Naval Hospital where his wounds were treated and he returned to duty.

For his bravery on this patrol, Lieutenant Graves received the Congressional Medal of Honor. Since he was killed in action, the Vice President of the United States, Spiro T, Agnew, presented the award to his family on December 2, 1969. Honeycutt received the Navy Cross. This was also presented posthumously to his family, since he was KIA. Corporal Thompson and PFC Lopez received the Silver Star posthumously. The Bronze Star was presented to Lance Corporal Emrick's family. Of the eight members of *Box Score* that went out on patrol that February 15th, only 3 survived.

Chapter 11 - Team *Breaker*

Sgt. James N. Tycz was winding down his tour in Vietnam. In fact, in a few days, this 22 year-old veteran would be leaving Alpha Company, 3rd Recon Battalion for home and a well-earned leave. He had one last assignment though. A new lieutenant, Second Lt. Heinz Ahlmeyer, arrived recently at Khe Sanh Combat Support Base. Since the lieutenant would be taking over as team leader for team *Breaker*, Sgt. Tycz planned to see the lieutenant got a proper introduction to the bush and the methods of patrolling in this area.

Sgt. Tycz could have gotten out of this mission, had he wanted to; but he felt a personal responsibility to the other members of the team. The other members of the team included Corpsman Malcolm T. Miller, radio operator, PFC Steven Lopez and riflemen, Lance Corporal Samuel A. Sharp, Jr., Clarence Carlson, and Carl Fiery. Soon two members of team *Breaker* would earn the Navy Cross and a third the Silver Star.

HM3 "Mac" Miller, came from Tampa, Florida. He was

popular with the girls in high school. His older sister, Sandra claims, "He had a girlfriend for every hour of the day."

Corpsman Malcolm T. Miller

She notes, "He used to keep a bottle of Brut on the dashboard of his family's green 1963 Plymouth Valiant, just in case he needed to splash on more during the course of the evening. If he had two dates scheduled for one night, he'd rush home to change between them."

At 16, Mac fell in with some bad companions. These

"friends" stole a car without his knowledge and invited Mac along for a ride. All the occupants in the car were arrested. Mac, being the oldest of the bunch, drew the most severe punishment. The judge hearing his case gave him a choice of military service or jail. Mac chose to enlist in the Navy and became a Corpsman.

He did well in Corpsman school and it aroused an interest in him to become a doctor when his service with the Navy was complete. He served on the USS Repose for a year. Then, in 1966 was reassigned to duties with the Marine Corps. He arrived in Vietnam on March 10, 1967, aboard a troop ship. Mac chose duty with recon rather than an infantry unit on recommendation of another serviceman.

Steven Lopez, a 1966 graduate of Springbrook High in Silver Springs, Maryland was a relative newcomer also, having only been on two previous reconnaissance patrols. The home base for Alpha Company was currently Khe Sanh Combat Support Base. Khe Sanh was located near the border with Laos. The Communist forces took advantage of the fact the United States would not send forces into Laos. The NVA and Viet Cong used a road along the Laotian border to bring troops and supplies from North to South. General Westmoreland, then Commander of all American forces in Vietnam, felt that the base was an important barrier to prevent the Communists from carrying the fighting to the eastern coastal regions of Vietnam.

Khe Sanh also was located close to the Demilitarized Zone (DMZ). It was one of a line of bases established to thwart enemy infiltration from North Vietnam to the South. Military leaders felt that, without Khe Sanh, entire North Vietnamese Divisions would "pour down Route 9 (the major east-west highway below the DMZ) and four other natural approaches through the valleys and could overrun a chain of Marine positions; the Rockpile, Con Thien, Dong Ha, and Phu Bai to the east." From Khe Sanh the Marines could launch offensive operations against enemy positions south of the DMZ and east of the Laotian border. The job of the men of the 3rd Recon Battalion was to locate these positions.

About four in the afternoon of May 9, 1967, team *Breaker* was inserted by helicopter onto a hilltop in elephant grass approximately 20 miles south of the DMZ, seven miles northeast of Khe Sanh and 12 miles east of the South Vietnamese Laotian border. The chosen landing zone was in the open with the jungled Hill 665 rising above them. The team assumed their security perimeter as the insert helicopter group disappeared into the distance.

Sgt. Tycz began to move the team toward the cover of the jungle when the team discovered freshly turned dirt that indicated recent occupation by the enemy. Using their entrenching tools (a shovel that folds for easy packing) the team began to uncover additional evidence of enemy occupation. Disgustingly they uncovered places the enemy used for a toilet as well as fighting holes and bunkers. They spent considerable time doing this.

As dusk neared, Sgt. Tycz realized they had better locate a harbor site for the night. It was extremely dangerous to remain at an insert LZ. Tycz took Corpsman Miller and his two most experienced Marines, Carlson and Sharp to check out the finger of land they were on. He told Lt. Alhmeyer, PFC Lopez and PFC Friery to stay put. These three had the radios and grenade launcher. Lt. Alhmeyer, ignoring the requests of the two PFC's to stay and wait for Tycz to return, wandered off through the elephant grass.

When Tycz returned and found the lieutenant gone he was steamed! He was about to search for Alhmeyer, when the lieutenant returned. Tycz vented his anger by having "words" with Lt. Alhmeyer. After this initial exchange Tycz and Alhmeyer moved about ten to 15 meters from the rest of the team to study the maps. One of the team members said he heard what sounded like the two arguing. Apparently the lieutenant ended the argument by pulling rank and ordered the team to stay where they were for the night. The team took cover in the grass with each man to take his turn on radio watch while the others slept.

Shortly after midnight, L.Cpl. Carlson heard sounds of brush rustling near the team. As he roused the other team members, the sounds spread. It seemed NVA were approaching from every direction. Friery was still asleep when PFC Lopez opened fire on two NVA approaching the two of them. Firing right over Friery, the first rounds from Lopez's rifle struck the first NVA. This NVA soldier fell, mortally wounded, firing an automatic burst from his weapon. Lopez dropped the second enemy soldier before the NVA soldier could fire a shot. The enemy's burst of automatic fire struck both Lt. Alhmeyer and Sgt. Tycz. The Lieutenant moaned, signaling he had been badly hurt.

The rest of the team began throwing grenades at the enemy, who, by now were so close the team could hear the enemy cries of pain. The enemy began throwing grenades also, aiming at the sound of the wounded lieutenant. Sgt. Tycz, who had been on the radio, started grabbing the incoming grenades as they impacted and throwing them back at the enemy. One went off in the sergeant's hand, badly wounding him and Carlson who had come to assist Sgt Tycz.

The sergeant asked for morphine and Carlson administered the shot. Then Carlson tried to contact headquarters on the radio only to find the handset had been shot away from the radio. Carlson scrambled to the second radio only to find it out of commission also. Crawling around on his stomach, Carlson managed to piece together a working radio from the two. Contacting headquarters, he learned Sgt. Tycz had managed to get through before the first radio had been shot up and that help was on the way.

While Carlson was working on the radio, the NVA continued to pour on the automatic weapons fire with the worst of it coming from the east. Although the Marine team members were only a few meters apart, at this point none knew for sure which of them were alive or dead. Friery then saw Sharp fall, firing an automatic burst as he went down. Friery made his way over to Sharp and found his teammate dead with a bullet hole threw his head.

Carlson called for an artillery fire mission; but it had no effect. He passed the radio to Lopez who continued to call for artillery strikes. The artillery battery would only fire single rounds, however, in response to Lopez's direction. The battery wouldn't respond to his request to "fire for effect". (Note: "fire for effect" means the artillery battery fires a group of rounds after the person requesting artillery support determines the last "test" round landed sufficiently close to the enemy's position.) Perhaps, since the enemy soldiers were so close to the Marines, the battery commander was too concerned about hitting the team members.

After the first hour of contact, the team members Miller, Carlson, Lopez and Friery were the ones still alive. At this time, the first helicopters arrived. Diving into the valley, now illuminated by flares, the helicopter gunships spotted the team and the enemy only fifteen feet from the team. They began making passes, firing their machine guns into the NVA positions. These were followed by "Puff the Magic Dragon". "Puff" or "Spooky" as the airplane was also called, was a C-47 cargo plane specially equipped with machine guns capable of delivering 3,000 to 6,000 rounds a minute into a small area. When the plane banked and delivered the ordinance, it was a spectacle to be seen and deadly to anything in the target area.

Two CH-46's arrived after Puff. They were there to rescue the team. After several passes and guidance from the gunships, the CH-46 pilots located team *Breaker* on the edge of a bomb crater. Lt. Roberts, copilot of the first CH-46, describes how Major Colbert brought his helicopter down in an attempt to recover the team. In his own words:

"We approached the ground and came to hover over the lip of the bomb crater, at this instant, we began receiving fire from all directions. The aircraft seemed to shudder and then the major added power and moved off to the right and started climbing ...a round came up through the right heel rest and into my right foot..."[6]

Major Colbert managed to pull the helicopter away from the murderous gunfire. The crippled helicopter, with three wounded of the four crew aboard wounded, managed to hold together and land successfully at Khe Sanh.

As Major Colbert was conducting his rescue attempt, back on the ground "Doc" Miller was shot. The "Doc" was hit in the femur artery. As Lance Corporal Carlson assisted the Corpsman with his wounds, he heard a grenade land behind him. In an attempt to shield the Corpsman, Carlson rolled on top of the grenade, with the grenade under his back. The grenade didn't explode but the next one thrown at them wounded both Miller and Carlson. The Doc then asked Carlson to prop him up on his pack so he could defend their rear. When Carlson this, Doc Miller slumped over dead.

After another pass by Puff the Magic Dragon, another CH-46 arrived on the scene to attempt to rescue the team. This bird had Captain Looney in the pilot's seat and Lieutenant Roots as copilot. By this time, the helicopter gunships had expended their ammunition and couldn't assist the rescue effort. Captain Looney flew his helicopter in low then pulled up hovering near the bomb crater. He radioed the team asking for a strobe to pinpoint their position. Carlson heard the call for a strobe but had none so he tossed out a white phosphorus grenade instead. Because his throwing arm was wounded the grenade didn't travel far and went off just a little ways in front of him. Carlson began to pray.

Captain Looney brought the chopper in. As he did so, a grenade landed near Friery. He picked it up and threw it back. Then he was hit in the legs. Almost simultaneously, the NVA blasted out the windshield on the pilot's side of the helicopter. Captain Looney was mortally wounded. Sergeant Reese, the crew chief and Doc Bridges, a Corpsman on board were also wounded. Lt. Roots took over the controls, climbing away from the enemy gunfire on the ground. Captain Looney managed to pull himself from his seat and move to the rear of the aircraft. Another Marine onboard, Corporal Remo was assisting the crew chief and Corpsman. Lt. Roots called him forward. He told Remo to take the Captains seat and help pilot the helicopter. The Corpsman, who had been unconscious, came to and tended to the wounded Captain and crew chief. Lt. Roots managed to get the ship back to Khe Sanh and land it successfully. Captain Looney died of his wounds shortly after arriving at Khe Sanh.

Back at the firefight now only Lopez and Carlson were continuing the fight. Friery was unconscious. Carlson was shot again in the arm while trying to lob a grenade. He gave himself a shot of morphine, shortly after he was hit in the leg. At this point he lost his fear of death and only longed to take as many NVA as possible with him into the afterlife. To this end he called for another artillery fire mission; but no rounds came. Lopez by now had suffered wounds to both his abdomen and back. He prayed to God for assistance, then, experienced a rush of euphoria, and passed out.

At daylight, the new helicopter gunships arrived and relieved the ones on station. These helicopters were equipped with special guns that allowed them to deliver devastating fire to the enemy below. These were followed by jets, which dropped napalm on the NVA. In the elephant grass the napalm started a fire, which threatened to consume both the NVA and the Marines. For the next two hours, jets and helicopter gunships continually bombed and strafed enemy positions around the Marines.

At about 9:00 in the morning Cpl Ted Bizko, who

considered Sgt Tycz his best friend, gathered the 5 men on his team and boarded a CH-46 headed for besieged recon team. He told the helicopter pilot just to get them close enough that his team could jump off the tailgate. He also told the pilot that if it wasn't possible to extract *Breaker* his team would stay with team *Breaker*.

When they were getting close, the pilot signaled to Cpl. Bizko, who got his team to the back of the helicopter ready to go. As the CH-46 neared the ground, it started receiving heavy hits. A 50-caliber machine gun bullet passed through the deck of helicopter right next to Cpl Biszko. Next the bird started to roll as though it was out of control. The pilot was forced to abort the attempt; but managed to hold the chopper together long enough to land at Khe Sanh. When the '46 landed the team, afraid the helicopter would blow up, scrambled off.

The company commander met Biszko at the LZ and directed him to another chopper ready to take off. This time Biszko instructed the pilot to make an attempt to insert the team following a bombing run by the jets, using the dust created by the exploding bombs as cover. This attempt failed also. The helicopter started taking hits. A fuel line was hit, soaking the team with fuel. Then the CH-46 began to move erratically. Again they had to return to Khe Sanh.

Back at the battle site, Lopez and Friery had returned to the conscious world, and, along with Carlson, were desperately fighting to survive. The gunships continued to support them, leaving only to refuel and reload ammunition, at which time other gunships would take their place. Now the grass fire was growing and threatening to engulf the team. One NVA popped up in the grass. Lopez caught him in his sights and dropped the soldier who fell into the fire.
At Khe Sanh, Major Charles Reynolds, pilot for the 3rd Marine Division Commanding Officer, arrived in an unarmed Huey helicopter. The major and pilots from two other CH-46

helicopters decided to use the Huey to extract the team while the other two helicopters acted as decoys. When they arrived at the battle site, the gunships led Major Reynolds in but heavy gunfire drove them off. They tried again, coming in from a different direction. Again they had to abort. Now the 46s made their fake runs, receiving small arms fire as they approached. With the Huey and gunships in a tight formation, the three helicopters made a third try. Carlson describes what happened next:

> "When the chopper came in from the east and came up from the bottom of the valley floor up to where we were. We spotted him and all three of us ran for the chopper. It didn't matter about the wounds-we ran." [7]

Two Marines aboard the Huey helped the wounded survivors of team *Breaker* board the aircraft. Friery was still half hanging off the helicopter as it took off. The Marines inside pulled him in.

For "extraordinary heroism" Sergeant Tycz and PFC Steven Lopez were later awarded the Navy Cross. Of course the award had to be presented to the family of Sergeant Tycz as he died during the fight and his body was never recovered. Likewise the bodies of Miller, Sharp and Lieutenant Ahlmeyer were never recovered. LCpl Carlson received the Bronze Star.

In 2003, a joint United States/Socialist Republic of Vietnam team returned to this hill in response to rumors that it was haunted. There they excavated and found 31 tooth fragments. Later analyses by a laboratory in Hawaii determined the teeth had come from the bodies of Sgt. Tycz, Mac Miller, Lt. Ahlmeyer, and L.Cpl. Sharp.

The area around Khe Sanh was to be a hot bed of enemy activity for some time to come. In early 1968, 20,000 NVA surrounded and lay siege to 6,000 Marines stationed there. The Marines held the base against repeated enemy attacks until the siege was lifted approximately two months later.

[6] *Never Without Heroes,* page 145
[7] *Never Without Heroes,* page 151

Chapter 12 – Clovis (Buck) Coffman

Clovis Coffman actually started his Marine Corps career in high school. He enlisted in the Marine Corps Reserve in 1949 while attending Craddock High School in Portsmouth, Virginia. He was a son of a Marine Colonel and nephew of a general officer, so his attraction to the Marine Corps may have involved family tradition. After graduating, he went on to become a full-fledged Marine just in time for the Korean War.

He was with the 1st Marine Division when they made an amphibious landing at Inchon, Korea. He also was with the 1st Marine Division at the Chosin Reservoir. The Chosin Reservoir campaign was perhaps one of the toughest campaigns the Marines ever faced. When the campaign began the Marines had the North Korean Communists on the run, heading toward the Yalu River, which separated North Korea from China. When the Marines reached the Chosin Reservoir in late November they didn't know they were in for a great surprise. During the night of November 27 – 28, 1950, twelve divisions of Communist Chinese began their assault on the 1st Marine Division. Before long they had the 1st Marine Division completely surrounded. To make matters worse, the weather turned bitterly cold. Twelve Chinese Communist divisions now surrounded the Marines. They had no choice but to fight their way through the Communists to Hungnam, a port city where they could be evacuated by ship. The trip took two weeks, fighting not only the Chinese, but frostbite as well. Since frostbite usually affects the hands and feet the most, it is particularly devastating to the infantryman who depends on his feet to get from one place to another and his fingers to fire his rifle.

Buck Coffman suffered the pain of frostbite, since he was part of the Division that fought their way to Hungnam. His feet were severely frostbitten. During the time he spent in Korea, he was also wounded 4 times and awarded the Silver Star.

In 1965, now a Gunnery Sergeant in the Marine Corps, Buck Coffman went to Vietnam for the first time. He was assigned to Company C, 1st Reconnaissance Battalion, 1st Marine Division. On October 10, 1966 he was confronted with another great challenge. He led a thirteen man patrol that had been assigned the mission of observing a valley near Long Bihn, Quang Ngai Province for enemy activity. That afternoon the patrol came under heavy small arms and grenade attack from an estimated 35 to 50 man enemy force. GySgt Coffman immediately positioned his men so they could effectively return fire on an enemy that out-numbered them. Buck Coffman repeatedly exposed himself to enemy fire by popping up to determine enemy locations so that he could direct the fire of his men.

During the enemy assault on this recon team, one of the Marines had been wounded and separated from the others. Sergeant Coffman rushed to aid the wounded Marine. In his effort he was wounded, but he was able to kill three of the enemy as he strove to reach the wounded Marine. He then managed to assist this Marine back to their defensive perimeter. Next the patrol's medical corpsman received disabling wounds. Because of this, Sergeant Coffman had to administer first aid to four of the team members. With air support now on station, Sergeant Coffman directed fixed wing and armed helicopter assaults against the enemy positions with devastating accuracy. The air support was so effective that helicopters were able to land and extract all the team. Even though Sergeant Coffman was wounded, he was one of the last Marines taken by a helicopter. He and another Marine defended the landing zone until the rest of the team were on the helicopters. The fighting got so intense Coffman and the other Marine fought hand-to- hand, killing four of the enemy before boarding the aircraft themselves. For his actions on this patrol, Gunnery Sergeant Coffman was awarded the Navy Cross.

After Vietnam, Coffman's next assignment was to Quantico, Virginia, to assist with training future officers. By this time Clovis Coffman had been promoted to 2nd Lieutenant. Major General Nickerson, Commanding General of the 1st Marine Division promoted Coffman to an officer based on his action in Vietnam. At Quantico, he served with Major Alex Lee and was soon to serve under Major Lee back in Vietnam again.

In August 1969, Lieutenant Coffman was assigned to 3rd Force Reconnaissance Company. The same month Major Lee arrived to take command of the company. At that time 3rd Force was acting as an additional company for the 3rd Reconnaissance Battalion. As a result, the company's morale suffered. The Battalion had taken over the company's special equipment and the company had acquired a reputation of being the least competent of the companies in 3rd Recon Battalion. Major Lee with the assistance of Lieutenant

Coffman immediately set about to restore the pride and special identity of the 3rd Force Recon company.

In September 1969, Lt. Coffman, whom Major Lee dubbed "Igor," made an impression the troops of 3rd Force would not soon forget. The company received an assignment to do a bomb damage assessment following a B-52 bomber strike south of the Ben Hai River. Bomb damage assessments were particularly dangerous assignments. The enemy knew that ground troops would come to assess how effective the bombing was on the target area. The enemy also favored making a camp in a bombed out area on the theory that the bombed out area would not likely be chosen as a target a second time.

Igor was with the team chosen to conduct the bomb damage assessment; but as an observer. Corporal Heffington, an American Indian from Oklahoma was the team leader.

Major Lee and the other military commanders involved did their best to carefully coordinate the bombing run and subsequent assessment to minimize the amount of time the recon team would have to spend on the ground. Major Lee, flying in the aircraft with an air observer, had a good position to watch the action of the aircraft at least as the mission unfolded. The B-52's, flying at an altitude above the clouds, were never seen. A radio message was the only notice that the bombs were on their way. As the earth below erupted in a series of clouds of dust and smoke, the CH-46 helicopter carrying the recon team was already preparing to set down by the first bomb crater.

Once on the ground, Corporal Heffington began the process of reporting the conditions in the bomb craters, which would tell the military strategists how successful the bombing mission had been. As Heffington's team was examining the first several bomb craters, Cobra gunships, which escorted the team's helicopter to the bomb site, reported they had taken fire from enemy forces on a small ridge roughly one thousand meters north of the team. The pilot of the OV-10 aircraft Major Lee rode in made a low pass over the same area and received small arms fire also. Major Lee got on the radio and told Heffington about the enemy activity. About thirty minutes later, Heffington reported his team was receiving such heavy small arms fire that he would have to abort the mission and requested extraction.

At this point Lt. Coffman took charge. First he went from man to man calming each one and pointing out enemy targets. Next he grabbed Corporal Heffington, pulled him to the edge of the bomb crater, stood up and said:

"Now, Chief, I want you to stand up here with me so I can teach you something important." [8]

Reluctantly Corporal Heffington stood up. Lt. Coffman pointed out an NVA in the brush. When the soldier moved, Igor shot the NVA in the head. Afterwards he instructed the other members of the recon team in the crater:

"You never use only one round. Got that? Never! Never ever shoot anyone once. Always make sure that once he is down, he stays down." [8]

Then Igor continued to fire from the standing position, dropping another NVA soldier. Then he turned to Corporal Heffington and announced; "Okay, Chief, school's out. You can get down now." [8]

F-4 Phantom jets then arrived, attacking the NVA positions with bombs and napalm. The F-4 attacks reduced the fire the recon team was receiving to about 10% of the previous level. The Cobra's then went to work on the enemy, allowing a CH-46 to drop in the crater where Heffington's team was and successfully extract the team. The seven man recon team returned to base without any casualties.

I   n February of 1970, 3rd Force Recon, now the only reconnaissance unit operating in the area formerly patrolled by the 3rd Reconnaissance Battalion, now was involved in tracking the movements of a NVA regiment. After a bombing run in the western Ashau Valley, Major Lee decided to send Lt. Coffman in to try and determine what the NVA were up to. A-6 aircraft had bombed the area earlier. When Coffman's team landed, Igor immediately assessed that the bombs had inflicted significant damage on the NVA.

Before long, the NVA made their appearance. They assaulted Coffman's team with heavy machine-gun fire from two directions. Cobra helicopters tried to assist the team; but the NVA seemed bent on destroying the recon Marines. Still, Igor's team held on, firing back at their attackers.

Meanwhile, a UH-1H helicopter, piloted by Army Chief Warrant Officer Kiersley, went in to attempt a rescue of the team. With the help of another UH-1H helicopter and some Cobras, Kiersley managed to maneuver his helicopter into a position where Coffman's team could board. Of course, Lt. Coffman was the last one on board. As the extract helicopter took off, the recon Marines assisted the helicopter gunner in providing suppressive fire. This was necessary because the NVA attempted to storm the extract helicopter.
The event was so hair-raising that Kiersley broke out in hives!

Lieutenant Coffman went on to achieve the rank of Major before he retired from the Marine Corps. Upon his death, the Secretary of the Navy promoted him to Lt. Colonel Coffman, which was quite unusual. However, he was an unusually brave and courageous man.

[8] *Force Recon Command: A Special Marine Unit in Vietnam*

Chapter 13 - Team *Deer Fern*

Jerry Miller was shocked when Corporal Farrell announced Miller would take over as team leader of *Deer Fern*. Lance Corporal Miller had only newly arrived in Vietnam. On his first patrol, Corporal Miller assigned him to be Assistant Patrol Leader; but that patrol never got off the helicopter, having encountered enemy fire as the first team members exited the helicopter ramp. Those team members quickly returned and the helicopter returned to base at Quang Tri. The upcoming patrol would only be L.Cpl. Miller's second since arriving in Vietnam! How could he possibly be prepared for this awesome responsibility?

Jerry Miller came from a small town, Glenwillard, Pennsylvania, located about 20 miles northwest of Pittsburgh. The house didn't even have a bathroom or running water. Many of the men from the community of about 100 worked in the steel mills nearby. Jerry's father and mother divorced when he was too young to remember his father.

One of the youthful pleasures Jerry enjoyed was

hunting. Jerry and his best friend Jackie learned the skill of archery from an accomplished outdoorsman in town named Skibow Skopinski.

Jerry and Jackie nearly got in trouble on their first hunt. Each of them bagged what they thought to be a duck, which turned out to be a couple of pet geese of one of the ladies in the community. They had kept their hunting expedition quiet because their grandmother, who looked after them while their mother was at work, didn't approve of the boys having bows and arrows. Their mother, however, caught them with the dead geese. She had suspected the boys might be out hunting so, when she learned that duck hunting season just opened, she skipped work to check up on them. Fortunately, she helped them bury the geese so the boys wouldn't have to face the wrath of the lady whose geese they killed.

When Jerry turned 18, he, was required to register with the Selective Service. Back then when one registered with the Selective Service, you were likely to be drafted into the Army. At the time Jerry had to register, the President of the United States was committing more and more troops to the conflict in Vietnam. To meet this commitment, the Selective Service had to increase the number of men being drafted. At that time, however, there were a number of ways for an 18 year old to avoid being drafted. Probably the most common way was to go to college. That usually meant the potential draftee was safe for four years until he graduated. Jerry had no plans to attend college, so he expected to be drafted soon.

Jerry's friends decided to take him to West Virginia to celebrate his 18th birthday. It was legal to drink at 18 in West Virginia. He got to drinking with his friends. Under the influence of alcohol, his buddies made a pact that they would all enlist in the Army the next day together since they would likely be drafted anyway. On their way to the Federal Building in Pittsburgh, PA, however, they met a Marine recruiter who convinced the group to enlist in the Marine

Corps. To Jerry's surprise, however, none of his buddies passed the entrance physical and mental examinations, and Jerry was soon off to Boot Camp at Parris Island, South Carolina. His friends had just pulled a practical joke on him and Jerry would have to accept the consequences.

After Boot Camp and a tour of duty in Guantanamo Bay, Cuba, Jerry Miller received orders to report to Camp Pendleton, California. At Pendleton, Jerry was assigned to Reconnaissance School. Here he learned the skills required of a Reconnaissance Marine in the mountains of Southern California. Jerry's squad excelled in map reading at this school, taking first place. In September of 1968, with Reconnaissance school completed, Lance Corporal Jerry Miller was on his way to Vietnam.

With Jerry Miller in charge of team *Deer Fern*, he now needed an assistant patrol leader (APL). He chose Henry Hames. Henry was from Portland, Oregon. He actually had been born in Dallas, Texas; but his dad decided to move to Oregon when Henry was in his early teens. In high school Henry didn't participate in sports because his father couldn't afford to pay for the insurance policies required to cover potential sports injuries.

In high school Henry fell in love with a girl named Brenda. They married young. Henry was 19 and Brenda 16. Brenda soon delivered a son, Shawn. As a young father, Henry was hard pressed to provide for his wife and son. He started working as a busboy in a restaurant. At this time, probably because of the low wages a busboy could make as well as the desire to serve his country, Henry made the decision to join the Marine Corps. By September 1968 he was a member of 3rd Squad, 3rd Platoon, Alpha Company, 3rd Reconnaissance Battalion.

Another member of team *Deer Fern* came from Portland, Oregon; but with a vastly different background. Born in Cuba, Jorge Nunez managed to escape the dictatorial communist regime of Fidel Castro in 1962. Alone, at age 14 he made his way to the United States. As a refugee, Catholic Charities took responsibility for him and relocated him to Portland, Oregon with a foster family. In Portland Jorge Nunez attended Central Catholic High School and graduated in 1967. Seeking adventure, Jorge enlisted in the Marine Corps. After boot camp, Infantry Training Regiment, and Basic Infantry Training School, the Marine Corps offered Jorge an opportunity to become a scout-sniper or a recon Marine. Since scout-snipers operated in teams of two and recon Marines in teams of at least six, Jorge chose recon. He felt his chances of survival were better with the larger numbers. When he joined team *Deer Fern* in 1968, he had already been wounded in combat, so he was a veteran warrior in every sense of the word.

The other members of team *Deer Fern* included Gary Stepp, the radioman, Floyd Hatfield, an American Indian, Campbell, a street-wise tough from Washington, D.C. and Tom Murray who became a close friend of Jerry Miller. To attend to their medical needs, the team had Corpsman Ray Minks.

Team *Deer Fern*, with Jerry Miller as patrol leader, spent their first patrol at a radio relay site named *Romeo*. After that assignment, the team was ordered in early October 1968 to Cua Viet to assist an Army unit that was having some difficulty locating a NVA unit which had been mortaring the Army unit on a fairly regular basis. The attacks killed nine men from the Army unit and wounded fifteen more. By luck rather than skill, *Deer Fern*, located an NVA ammo dump. They had the 16-inch cannons of the battleship *New Jersey* to provide the kind of support they would normally get from a Marine artillery battery.

After chasing the NVA up and down the coast night after night, the team hadn't been able to fix the enemy's position. With a feeling of frustration and curiosity at what the *New Jersey's* guns could do, Jerry called a fire mission on a location he only hoped was enemy occupied. When the rounds from the *New Jersey's* guns impacted, a series of secondary explosions indicated the shells from the *New Jersey* had landed on a NVA ammunition dump. The *New Jersey* continued to pound the position until nearly 400 rounds had been spent. For their success in locating the NVA ammo dump, all the team members were promoted one grade. They also were invited by the *New Jersey* to spend three days aboard as guests.

However the NVA mortar fire hadn't been silenced. On a later patrol, team *Deer Fern* located the mortar fire coming from a cave in the dunes along the coast. Corporal Miller felt he could easily destroy the enemy position with one round from the *New Jersey* The Lieutenant commanding them, however, wanted to lead an attack on the position in revenge for the casualties the enemy had inflicted on his company. He ordered *Deer Fern* to fall back to the beach and wait for him to arrive.

The next morning, the lieutenant arrived with fifty men and an Amtrak (An Amtrak is an amphibious assault vehicle. Its main use is to haul Marines from a ship anchored off shore to the beach. The vehicle can travel in water and on land.) The lieutenant jumped off the Amtrak and met with Corporal Miller. After Cpl. Miller showed the lieutenant where the NVA position was located on his map, his men assaulted the NVA position.

In the resulting firefight, two of the lieutenant's men were wounded. This so angered the lieutenant that he ordered the Amtrak to cross the Ben Hai River to chase a single NVA soldier whom they spotted crossing the river with a mortar tube on his shoulder. Cpl. Miller reminded the lieutenant his men would be crossing into North Vietnam. The lieutenant told Jerry he would chase the guy with the mortar tube to Hanoi if necessary. Jerry calmly told the lieutenant he could

could get the guy with fire support from the *New Jersey*. The lieutenant ordered Cpl. Miller to proceed with the fire mission. Jerry called it in and the *New Jersey's* rounds were right on target.

Following the elimination of escaping mortar man, Jerry went to work on the sand dunes where his team had located the NVA mortar position. It took only six rounds to completely level the dunes. Meanwhile the lieutenant's troops that had crossed the border into North Vietnam found a series of caves the enemy had been using for a field hospital. Cpl. Miller sent Floyd Hatfield into the cave and the Marine emerged with boxes of medical supplies that had been supplied by Jane Fonda. (Jane Fonda was a popular movie star at the time. She liked to draw attention to herself by participating in antiwar activities. She even went to North Vietnam. Many in the United States considered her actions treason; but she was never prosecuted for treason.)

After examining the interconnecting series of caves, Jerry Miller blew up the entrance to the cave with a Light Antitank Assault Weapon (LAAW). He couldn't call another fire mission because President Johnson had just ordered all bombing of North Vietnam to cease. (Both President Johnson and President Nixon halted bombing of the North at various times during the war as gesture to encourage the North Vietnamese to negotiate peace terms.) This bombing halt meant the *New Jersey* could no longer fire on targets north of the Ben Hai River.

On December 4, 1968, team *Deer Fern* was inserted by helicopter into an area located about midway between Khe Sanh and Quang Tri located in the Ashau valley. At the time, the reconnaissance patrols had found the enemy appeared to be preparing for another major offensive during the holidays, similar to the Tet offensive of early 1968. Jerry Miller, by this time had been on double the number of patrols than the average team member. Fatigued, he asked the platoon commander, Lieutenant Bailey if someone else could lead the patrol. Lieutenant Bailey agreed and declared that Henry Hames, the assistant patrol leader was ready to take out his first patrol. Jerry told the lieutenant he didn't think Henry was quite ready to take over as leader; but Lt. Bailey stood fast to his decision.

At 9:30 a.m. on December 4th, team *Deer Fern* began its patrol with Lance Corporal Hames as team leader. The area where the team was to conduct the patrol had steep slopes with a heavy canopy formed by the trees, thick underbrush on hilltops and scattered areas of elephant grass.

At one o'clock in the afternoon, the team made their first enemy sighting. They observed an enemy 50-caliber machine gun position. The enemy was firing at a helicopter. L.Cpl. Hames called in a fire mission on the machine gun position. The artillery rounds landed on target, and four secondary explosions informed the team the fire mission was a success. The team continued their patrol until dark when they selected a harbor site for the night.

About 1 o'clock in the morning, the team heard movement and voices some distance from their position. The team called a fire mission, after which it got quiet again until 5 a.m. when the team spotted a flashlight and called a fire mission on that location. By 11 a.m. team *Deer Fern* had resumed patrolling when they sighted smoke from an enemy campfire. Again, they called a fire mission. The artillery strike resulted in secondary explosions that appeared to indicate the strike had created a fire on the enemy's ammunition cache. The team observed two VC or NVA men attempt first to put out the fire and then they packed up a black box. By this time an air observation plane was now in the air over the site. The AO ran two airstrikes on the enemy position, causing two more secondary explosions and an additional fire.

At about twenty after two in the afternoon, the enemy had located the team and began firing at them from two separate locations. L.Cpl. Hames directed AO strikes on both positions. One enemy soldier was killed and team *Deer Fern* managed to break contact. At this time, a reaction force was inserted to assist team *Deer Fern*. Then the AO ran another airstrike in the vicinity that resulted in more secondary explosions. The reaction force located *Deer Fern* and, with the team, moved to a location where they set up for the night.

About 9 p.m., the team heard two dogs and called a fire mission on the location of the sound; but heard the dogs again about an hour later. At midnight, the enemy hit *Deer Fern's* position with 20 rounds of 60-mm mortars, small arms fire and grenades. Henry Hames was killed and the other six team members wounded. The team requested a medical evacuation. At 1 a.m., with helicopter gunships providing covering fire, *Deer Fern* was extracted.

For his action that night Henry Hames was awarded the Silver Star posthumously. On December 7, 1968, Alpha Company, 3rd Recon Battalion held a memorial service for Henry. The company gave him a 21-gun salute with his rifle stuck in the ground and his helmet on top of the rifle. They sounded *Taps* and all the company saluted.

This patrol also was the end of team *Deer Fern*. A new lieutenant, Lt. Joiner, combined the remnants of the 3rd Squad, 3rd Platoon with 2nd Squad, 3rd Platoon and formed a new team with the call sign *Iceboat*. Corporal Jerry Miller became the patrol leader of this team.

Chapter 14 - Team *Flight Time*

For Billy Buck it was "Déjà vu" all over again. Bill's first patrol had been on Hill 471 and now he was back again. By this time, he was a seasoned veteran of Delta Company, 3rd Recon Battalion.

Billy grew up in Fayetteville, North Carolina. Under the guidance of a father who became a Master Sergeant in the Army as well as a Scoutmaster, Bill learned the outdoor crafts of a Boy Scout. In fact he achieved the highest rank, Eagle Scout. Even though Bill's dad was a career Army soldier, Bill chose to join the Marines because he perceived the Marine Corps to be the best. For the same reason, he chose to be a Reconnaissance Marine. He felt they were the best within the Marine Corps.

Bill had already done a full 13-month tour in Vietnam. He could have returned to the United States and trained future Reconnaissance Marines at a base like Camp Pendleton, California. There he would have weekends free to surf the beaches of Southern California or pursue the young ladies who frequented the beaches. After all, he was a handsome man, and likely to attract many women. Instead, Bill chose to extend his tour in Vietnam for an additional 6 months. By volunteering for an extension, he received 30 days leave. This he used to visit his parents and girlfriend in Fayetteville. Bill's mother was somewhat upset to learn of his decision to extend his tour in Vietnam. Her woman's intuition gave her a strange sense of foreboding.

Nevertheless, Bill Buck returned to his unit at Quang Tri June 1st of 1968. Bill volunteered to lead team *Flight Time*. The team's Assistant Patrol Leader (APL), Stan Kozlowski, had just left on training assignment, leaving the team without a patrol leader. Bill was the logical choice. After 13 months of patrolling, he had experience as a pointman, radioman, and, most importantly, patrol leader. Cpl. Buck was anxious to resume his duties as a patrol leader. He knew he had the one thing that few Marines could provide at this time and place – experience.

One of Bill's team members was Private First Class Robert Pearcy. Pearcy came from the opposite end of the United States. Bob Pearcy grew up in the relatively tight-knit community of Big Bear Lake, California. Big Bear Lake was fairly well-removed from the war. Perhaps Bob could have found a way to avoid military service. After all, he had a lot going for him. He had a girlfriend, Debbie, who enjoyed spending time with him. They hung out at a local teenage nightclub called the "Sugar Shack". They would also go boating, to the drive-in movies, or just for walks along the lake.

Then there were the dances. Debbie liked to meet Bob at the "Sugar Shack" for the dances. Being pretty, however, Debbie was often asked by others to dance. In fact there was one boy who constantly badgered her to dance with him. Bob came to Debbie's rescue, telling the guy to leave her alone, which he did.

Debbie, however, just couldn't comprehend Bob Pearcy's decision to join the Marine Corps. He tried to explain to her, "I have to fight for our freedom." Debbie told him he was an "idiot" and "stupid". Nevertheless, Bob followed through with his commitment to the Marine Corps.

Bob Pearcy did have aspirations beyond the Marine Corps. He expressed to Debbie his desires to be involved with kids. Apparently he wanted to be a teacher at some time in the future.

PFC Robert Pearcy

In Vietnam, Bob wrote to Debbie about the conduct of the war. He said, "If the Government let the Marines do what they were trained to do, the war would last only 30 days." He felt that "Big Business" kept the war restricted in scope.

Corporal William Buck's other patrol members were 1st Lieutenant Maurice O'Connor, Lance Corporal Warner Barniz, PFC Alonzo Skaggs, and Cpl. Martin Wellman. Apparently Lieutenant O'Conner was new to recon and was learning from Corporal Buck. It was not unusual for a lieutenant newly arrived in Vietnam to make his first patrol where the team leader was an enlisted man. In Vietnam, experience could mean the difference between life and death and it was best to have an experienced man as team leader.

On June 2, 1969, Team *Flight Time* was inserted near

Hill 471, a short distance north and east of Khe Sanh. Shortly after insertion, they came across an enemy campsite. The team reported finding cooking gear still hot, helmets and fresh banana peels. Ten meters from this site, *Flight Time* found a bunker that they assessed could have been used as an observation post. In addition, the team found: two bags of potatoes, two bags of rice, two helmets, one cartridge belt, one first aid kit, one belt, one pair of tennis shoes, one shirt, and one magazine for an AK-47 rifle, two bush hats, six fragmentation grenades, and American C-rations.

Record of the activities of *Flight Time* then skips to 5:50 p.m. on June 3, 1969. At this time the team reported seeing five enemy soldiers after setting into their harbor site. The harbor site that night was at the same location where the team had been inserted the day before. It is something of a mystery why the team patrol report has no entries between 9:40 a.m. on June 2nd and 5:50 p.m. on June 3rd. It is also a mystery why *Flight Time* chose a harbor site at the same map coordinates where they had been inserted. As noted in earlier stories in this book, it was standard procedure for recon patrols not to stay too close to an insert LZ. Nevertheless, the team took no action against the enemy soldiers they'd spotted and bedded down for the night.

At 2:50 in the morning of Jun 4th, *Flight Time* started receiving small arms fire and Chi-Com (Chinese-Communist manufactured) grenades. They reported one Marine dead, one seriously wounded and four others with minor wounds. Naturally, the team requested an emergency extraction.

At 3:05, an Air Observer arrived on station and reported that enemy assailants were attacking the team from approximately 10 meters on all sides. Following the arrival of the AO, the team requested the assistance of a reaction force. At 3:15, the Air Observer ran out of ammunition and could no longer provide fire support. Five minutes later the AO lost communication with the team.

By 4:00 a.m. the reaction force was airborne and on the way to rescue the besieged team. The patrol leader of the team *Deer Fern*, (mentioned in a previous chapter), happened to be on the 12-man reactionary force sent to help *Flight Time*. This was Corporal Jerry Miller. He describes his arrival at Hill 471 as follows:

> Doc Morrow to see if any of the men were still alive. A Chi-Com grenade or RPG (rocket propelled grenade) exploded on the side of the chopper as it lifted off. Our M-79 man, Cliff Atcheson was in the doorway exiting the chopper as it bounced from the explosion. At the time I wasn't aware of what had happened. It wasn't until we were waiting for extraction that we discovered Cliff's absence. We called into the dark night his name when he crawled into out perimeter. He had fallen some 20 feet from the departing CH-46, and was knocked unconscious. He remained that way through a ferocious firefight that continued for over an hour. We set up a 20' perimeter waiting for the second chopper to bring in the other six men of the reactionary team. …. Donald Simpson and I carried the bodies (of team *Flight Time*) to a bomb crater, as Doc worked on one Marine who was still alive. He died in Doc's arms from a massive chest wound. Doc also was in shock from the sight of a fellow corpsman he knew that lay dead. All the bodies were riddled from close fire and were stripped of their shirts and boots. Many had deep gashes from knife wounds which meant they went hand-to-hand with the enemy."

Five of team *Flight Time* lay in a trench. The sixth, Corporal Buck, was approximately 10 meters down the hill. He died with his K-Bar knife in his hand, apparently engaged in hand-to-hand fighting against an enemy who had overwhelmed him. The reaction team assessed that the main enemy force came up the northeast side of the hill, hitting the

Marines with satchel charges, Chi-Com grenades, Bangalore torpedoes and small arms fire. The enemy had taken four of the team's M-16 rifles, the M-79 grenade launcher, and a 45-caliber pistol. The team member bodies were riddled with bullets and torn by explosives.

The enemy had left behind three packs, a rocket-propelled grenade launcher with four rounds, and some assorted mess, medical gear and clothing. Apparently, the reaction team had arrived before the NVA could recover everything of value.

As the reaction team Corpsman bagged the bodies of team *Flight Time* for extraction and to be returned to the United States for burial, the NVA opened up with AK-47 rifle fire on the reaction force. Corporal Miller returned fire from his M-60 machine gun and threw all his grenades at the enemy. Out of the blue, two F-4 Phantoms arrived and assaulted the enemy positions with 30mm cannon fire, followed by the dropping of napalm. Meanwhile the rest of the reaction force prepared to spend the night on the hill, setting claymore mines along a defensive perimeter.

Fortunately, a CH-46 managed to land and recover the reaction force as well as the bodies of *Flight Time*. The dead team members were returned to their hometowns for burial with full military honors. At Big Bear Lake, Robert Pearcy was buried at Victor Valley Cemetery on a hill. His girlfriend notes his favorite song had been "Fool on the Hill" by the Beatles.

CHAPTER 15 - Team *Perspective 2* - Stirring up a Hornets Nest

Corporal David Freeman looked at the mission operation order given him. His team, *Perspective 2*, was to: "Conduct reconnaissance and surveillance in assigned zone to determine enemy activity. Engage enemy with supporting arms and establish ambushes of opportunity. Make every effort to capture a prisoner. Plot HLZ's for future operations."

The brass was expecting the team to mix it up with the enemy, hence the orders to "Engage enemy with supporting arms." So seven Marines and a Corpsman were going out into the badman's territory even though 3rd Recon Battalion patrols had been making increasing contact with the enemy, meaning NVA numbers were on the rise. It was recon's job to locate the enemy; but to pick a fight with them on their own turf was probably not the wisest thing for an eight-man team to do.

Nevertheless, orders were orders, and on February 26, 1967, Corporal Freeman and team *Perspective 2* were deep in the grass of the valley of the Song Cam Lo River starting a patrol that would be one the Marine Infantry Commanders in the area would not soon forget.

He had a good team. Ted Colschen was the radioman, then there was Shaw, Roland, Prather, Zamaites, and "Butch" Graciano. Freeman was from the south having graduated from Forest Hills High School in Marshville, North Carolina in 1965. Colschen, on the other hand, came from a moderately sized Iowa town on the Mississippi river, named Muscatine

He graduated from Muscatine High in 1964, just as things were heating up in Vietnam. He was later drafted into the Marine Corps. The Marine Corps was normally only composed of those who voluntarily enlisted. During the Vietnam War, however, as more and more troops were committed to the conflict and casualties increased, the Marines suffered manpower shortages and a small percentage of the men drafted for military service were sent to the Marines to fill the deficit. Ted volunteered for recon however, while sailing for Vietnam, as they called for volunteers while he was onboard the ship. After disembarking at Phu Bai, he went to Dong Ha where he joined the 2nd Squad, 1st Platoon, Company D, 3rd Reconnaissance Battalion.

Thirty minutes into the patrol, *Perspective 2* received four rounds of carbine fire. No one was injured and the sniper stopped shooting, so the patrol continued its mission. They found a trail, which appeared to have been used within the past 2-3 hours and began to follow it. It was littered with torn up propaganda leaflets, prepared by friendly forces to try to encourage the enemy soldiers to defect. A couple of hours, later the team found what appeared to be an entrance to a tunnel; but it didn't appear to have been used recently. About half an hour later the team heard about a dozen voices. They called an artillery fire mission. After the first round landed, the team no longer heard voices or any sound of movement so they didn't ask for additional rounds.

At 9:00 on February 27th, *Perspective* 2, after crossing a couple of small streams, found a trail, running southeast to northwest. It was 2 feet wide with fresh tennis shoe tracks. Then, at 10:00 a.m., the team made contact with four NVA soldiers while moving northwest along a trail. Both sides fired at each other, with the Marines managing to kill one of the NVA soldiers. Soon additional small arms fire erupted from the enemy position, suggesting the first NVA the Marines had encountered were being reinforced by an estimated company of enemy soldiers. The Marines immediately took defensive action. They broke contact and withdrew to the east, finding a spot where they could take advantage of concealing foliage and call an artillery fire mission on in the enemy. As the artillery shells began to land, the team heard a group of about 30 to 50 NVA pass by within about 20 feet of their position. What team *Perspective* 2 didn't know at the time was they had run into point scouts for a regiment of NVA!

The infantry unit, Lima Company, 3rd Battalion, 4th Marine Regiment was dispatched to assist the recon team. This company would have had between 150 and 200 men at the time; but it was reinforced with a platoon of tanks. This infantry unit was only 5,000 meters from the besieged recon team; but had to move through heavy brush, which retarded their movement. Before long, Lima Company ran into NVA and soon was engaged in heavy fighting. On top of that, one of the tanks had thrown a track and the company was forced to remain where they were and protect it.

Colonel John Lanigan, Commander of the 3rd Marine Regiment, ordered Companies G (Golf Company) and Company F (Foxtrot Company), and the Battalion Headquarters Company to assist the recon team. The three companies, which were part of 2nd Battalion of the 3rd Marine

Regiment were then located at Camp Carroll which was about 7,000 meters from the team. The 2nd Battalion, 3rd Marine Regiment had been in the process of loading on a ship for Okinawa. Foxtrot Company was only at half strength.

Team *Perspective* 2 was fighting off the NVA alone until about midnight, when Golf Company, Led by Captain Carl Bockewitz arrived and linked up with them. Captain Bockewitz established a defensive perimeter and stayed there for the night.

The next morning, Lieutenant Colonel Ohanesian, the Commander of 2nd Battalion, 3rd Marines, started off to link up with Golf Company with F Company and his Headquarters Company. Once they linked up with Company G, the Colonel planned for the combined forces to sweep east to Cam Lo, hoping to turn a defensive operation into an offensive one. Company L was to block the enemy's retreat from Colonel Ohanesian's advancing troops.

That was the plan; but the NVA didn't react as Colonel Ohanesian assumed. First they launched a vicious mortar attack on Company L. Striking from three sides, the NVA hit Lima Company with more than 150 82mm mortar rounds, automatic weapons, small arms, and an antitank rocket propelled grenade (RPG) fire. RPG rounds hit two of the tanks and set one on fire. The tanks crews, however managed to continue to support the infantry with their 50 caliber machine guns. Lima Company's Commander, Captain Hartney and his artillery forward observer, called in artillery fire to within 30 meters of the company's position. By 9:00 a.m., the morning of February 28th, after two and one-half hours of fighting, Marines had beaten back three enemy attacks.

Due to the unanticipated heavy assault on Lima Company, Colonel Lanigan ordered Ohanesian to link up with Lima Company instead of Company G. Under Colonel Ohanesian's command, Company F and the Battalion

Headquarters Company boarded trucks at Camp Carroll. They were then transported to Cam Lo, where they got off the trucks. By 10:30 a.m., Ohanesian's men had reached Company L. They'd used the sound of mortar fire to lead them to Lima Company. By this time, Company L had 4 dead and 34 wounded. The first action the combined forces took was to secure some high ground that could be used to evacuate the dead and wounded.

Meanwhile, *Perspective 2*, and Company G received orders to move some 2000 meters to the North and occupy Hill 124 where they would be able attack the NVA as they withdrew from the assault on Lima Company and Ohanesian's troops. Captain Bockewitz led his company up the hill; but soon found the NVA occupied it in well concealed positions. Heavy fighting ensued, and casualties piled up on both sides. Captain Bockewitz was one of those killed. Second Lieutenant, Richard C. Mellon, Jr., Bockewitz's executive officer took command of the company, as the fighting continued.

Back at Regimental Headquarters, Colonel Lanigan ordered Company M, 3rd Battalion, 4th Marines, to assist Company G. He put this unit under Colonel Ohanesian's command. Helicopters delivered Company M to Hill 162, which was immediately north of Company G's position. By 2:30 in the afternoon, Company M had landed on Hill 162 and started to move towards Company G.

At this time, Lt. Colonel Ohanesian started to lead his Headquarters Company and Company F toward Company G also. Lima Company and the serviceable tanks were to remain and protect the disabled ones.

Lt. Colonel Ohanesian's forces soon walked into a NVA ambush. Due to the terrain, the Marines were forced to walk single file and this made it easy for the NVA, located in well-concealed positions, to assault the Marines. The Marines found it impossible to establish fire superiority. At 3:10 p.m.,

Colonel Obanesian ordered his men to withdraw. Major Sheridan, Lt. Colonel Obanesian's executive officer describes the withdrawal as follows:

"…all radios had been hit and casualties continues to mount. Moving the dead and wounded out of the killing zone required feats of bravery beyond comprehension. The NVA were everywhere. Lieutenant Colonel Ohanesian was carrying the last of the wounded Marines towards the perimeter when an explosion mortally wounded him, three other Marines, and myself. None of us could walk and Marines had to leave the relative safety of their holes to get us."

Major Sheridan assumed command Ohanesian's troops. Despite being painfully wounded, directed the withdrawal of the troops to Lima Company's position. At this time he had 100 casualties on his hands and Sheridan requested emergency evacuation for them. The enemy assaulted Lima's position again, closing to within 20 meters. Helicopters arrived to evacuate the casualties; but couldn't land because of heavy fire in the landing zone.

As afternoon turned to evening, then to night, the enemy continued, intermittingly to overrun the Marines. Around midnight, Colonel Ohanesian died of his wounds. With the assistance of artillery and air strikes, the Marines manage to inflict enough casualties on the enemy that the NVA withdrew.

Earlier, at Regimental Headquarters, when Colonel Lanigan learned of the condition of the remnants of 2nd Battalion, 3rd Marines, he ordered his own executive officer, Lieutenant Colonel Delong to take command of what was left of this battalion. He also gave Lt. Colonel Delong operational control of 2nd Battalion, 9th Marine Regiment, which had recently arrived at Dong Ha. Company F from this battalion went by truck to Cam Lo, where it would start the overland journey on foot to reinforce the hard-pressed forces of

Ohanesian's Battalion. Colonel Delong attempted to land at the Lima Company position to take command. This was when the fighting was still intense and the helicopter transporting him couldn't land. Instead he ordered the pilot to take him to Cam Lo, where he took charge of Company F, 2nd Bn, 9th Marines, and began the march to Lima's position. At 3:40 in the morning, these troops arrived where Lima and 2nd Bn, 3rd Marines, had spent the night fighting off the NVA. Colonel Delong immediately began reorganizing the forces and preparing for evacuation of casualties.

By noon on March 1st, Company G, Company M, and *Perspective 2* arrived at Lima's position. With 2nd Bn, 9th Marines they searched the surrounding area and found a large amount of enemy equipment. The NVA were on the run now, however, and only Company M made several minor contacts with the enemy. What was left of 2nd, Battalion 3rd Marines left for the ship that would take them to Okinawa. The mission was over for *Perspective 2* also. For the rest of the troops under Delong's command, however there was unfinished business. Two new Marine Battalions were committed to pursuing the NVA regiment *Perspective 2* had stumbled into. The Marine infantry units continued the pursuit until March 3rd, when the enemy units became more exposed so that artillery and air strikes could be used more effectively.

It had taken five rifle companies to extract *Perspective 2* from the NVA they'd encountered. The team had really run into a "hornet's nest". The team, nevertheless, came out without casualty. Corporal Freeman was later awarded the Bronze Star for his actions on this patrol. In April 1967, the radioman, Colschen, was medevaced after being wounded in a subsequent patrol where he was one of five Marines and one Navy Corpsman wounded in action. Martin Prather gave his life for his country on a patrol in September 1967 when the NVA ambushed his team.

CHAPTER 16 - *Alpha-Deuce*

Private First Class James O'Leary looked out the rear of the helicopter as the ground approached. As pointman he would be the first to exit the helicopter. He could see the LZ was booby-trapped with punji sticks – not a good sign. Apparently the enemy expected this hill would be used as an LZ. Could there be additional surprises ahead? The pilot rotated the helicopter so that only the tailgate touched the ground. PFC O'Leary ran off the gate onto the ground, being careful to avoid the punji sticks. His first action was to clear them out of the way so the rest of the team could disembark. PFC Edward Smith came off next, followed by the rest of the team.

There were eleven of them. The most senior was Sergeant Robert Starbuck, the Platoon Sergeant for 2nd Platoon of Alpha Company, 1st Reconnaissance Battalion, which the Marines called Alpha Deuce. From Montgomery, New York, Sgt. Starbuck had been in the Marine Corps since March of 1961. Now, with nearly six years in the Marine Corps, he had completed a variety of assignments, including sea duty aboard the USS Little Rock, a drill instructor at Parris Island, South Carolina, and a Platoon Sergeant with two different infantry (grunt) units in Vietnam. He had been assigned to Alpha Deuce in December 1966.

The next most senior was Sgt. Robert Shafer. Sgt. Shafer was the squad and team leader. Robert Shafer came from the small town of Windsor, Illinois. One of four children, his cousin describes him as: "Full of spunk, curiosity, and drive." She also adds; "He had a spunky sense of humor, could be hot headed; after all he had two brothers to deal with."

Windsor was an agricultural community with almost no attractions for teenagers. The kids would hang out in the park, other friends' homes, or the pool hall. As a result, many looked forward to leaving Windsor upon graduation from high school.

While some might look forward to college, finding money to pay for this higher education wasn't easy. The other option was the military. Robert wanted to do more than stay in a small town so he chose to join the Marine Corps. His father was a World War II veteran and didn't want to see his son go off to the war in Vietnam. Nevertheless, Robert's dad signed the permission papers that would allow his son to join the Marines.

He'd started his tour in Vietnam with Company D, 1st Battalion, 7th Marine Regiment, a grunt unit. In December he was transferred to Chu Lai and duty with Alpha Company, 1st Recon.

The team radioman was Lance Corporal James Rowe. Jim was from Gettysburg, PA. He played football from 5th grade through his senior year in high school. He also participated in track and field, with the shot put and javelin throwing being his events. In grade school he liked playing the drums; but had to give it up because band practice conflicted with football practice. Jim's taste in music was varied. He liked rock n' roll, country, soul, ballads, and even some of the classics. He joined the Marines in spite of the fact his dad was retired from the Navy. He just couldn't fathom the idea of a watery grave or drowning in a burning oil slick at sea. After boot camp and radio operator school, he'd been assigned to the 1st Reconnaissance Battalion, where his radio skills were badly needed. He'd been with recon since June 11, 1966.

Jim's closest friend on the team was PFC Roger Smith. Roger's nickname was Boo Boo. He was from the South and went to boot camp at Parris Island. After basic and infantry training he was assigned to 1st Recon. Roger was one of two Smiths on the team. The other was PFC Edward Smith. Edward was from Easton, Massachusetts. He'd been a member of an undefeated high school football team and attended Northeastern University for a year. With anti-war protesters beginning to make their presence known, Ed decided he needed to go to Vietnam. He wanted to see first-hand what the war was all about. It so happened that he ended up in boot camp with Jim O'Leary and now they were on the same recon team.

The two new guys on the team were PFC Ray Chaplin and Robert Armitage. PFC Chaplin was from upstate New York. A quiet fellow, Chaplin seemed intent on learning the job he would have to perform throughout the rest of his tour in Vietnam. Bob Armitage came to the Marines from Everett Washington. He was born in Everett 23 August 1947, attended Everett schools and was a graduate of the Everett High School Class of 1965. One of his classmates describes him as "a cute shy boy."

Rounding out the team were L.Cpl. David "Frenchy" Verneyn, Private Charles Davis, and Klaus Urbaniak. Frenchy came from the Northeastern United States. Jim Rowe describes him as: "Self-confident – handsome enough to be in the movies." Charles Davis came from the south, having entered the Marine Corps in Birmingham, Alabama. Jim Rowe describes him as "Tall, skinny; but a strong 'farm' type." Klaus Urbaniak was a Midwesterner, having entered the Marine Corps in Minneapolis, Minnesota. Jim Rowe describes him as: "Down to earth, happy go lucky, a good man, common sense beyond his youth."

As Jim O'Leary led the patrol forward, he pondered the inconsistencies of this mission. They had been ordered to wear helmets and flak jackets. These weren't the normal apparel for a recon team. They added extra weight and the sound of brush scraping against this armor increased the chance the team would be discovered. In addition they were ordered to take along a M-60 machine gun. This gun and the additional ammunition was an additional burden. Shortly, Jim came upon a clearing. He noted that before them were two possibilities. The first was to climb a mountain, the second, to climb down the one they were on. He asked Sgt. Starbuck which option to choose. To Jim's surprise, Sgt. Starbuck ordered the team to dig foxholes in the clearing.

Sgt. Starbuck deployed the team in a "V" formation; placing the machine gun at the apex of the "V" which was located on a trail that led down from the hill they were on. Shortly before sunset, Corporal Shafer, while scanning the area below them through his binoculars, discovered three enemy soldiers looking back towards him through their binoculars. Corporal Shafer told Sgt. Starbuck about spotting the enemy soldiers; but the Sergeant decided to remain in their positions for the night.

The team ate chow, had a cigarette, and checked their weapons. They also talked among themselves in whispered tones. They enjoyed the sight of a beautiful sunset, then darkness and night descended with silence accompanying the night. As part of his preparation for night, Jim Rowe placed his ruck sack containing the PRC-25 radio against the only sizeable bush on the hilltop and directly to the left of Sgt. Starbuck. He had noted the location and adjusted the radio so he could rapidly contact the battalion or call for air or artillery support. Jim was confident he could locate the required radio frequencies in the dark without having to compromise their position by illuminating the radio with a flashlight or match or having to raise up to look down into the rucksack.

Sgt. Starbuck placed the team on 50% alert. This meant that half of the team could sleep while the other half had to stay awake. In either two or four hours those on watch would wake the other half of the team, who would stand watch so the first group could retire. Jim Rowe was one of the first who went to sleep.

About 9 or 9:30 that evening the enemy attacked. They hit the recon team first with fragmentary grenades. This was followed with rifle fire. During the initial assault they apparently shot Sgt. Starbuck in the head. Jim O'Leary heard the Sergeant moaning and went to assist him. The VC had also managed to capture the machine gun, killing Edward Smith and wounding Charlie Davis who fought them hand to hand before collapsing just within the point of the "V". Charlie, the machine gunner and Eddie Smith who was feeding the ammunition, were just overwhelmed by the VC who had two machine guns of their own. Sergeant Starbuck was able to force the VC to retreat with the cost of being seriously wounded himself. The VC managed to make off with the machine gun.

While this was going on, Jim Rowe awoke. He got on the radio and requested illumination rounds from their supporting artillery battery. He also reported the team's casualties to the battalion. The artillery battery responded almost immediately and soon flares were exploding overhead. Unfortunately, as Jim describes, "To my horror, the preset flare coordinates somehow positioned these air flares behind and seaward from the hilltop causing our "V" position to be flooded in the glare of light and shielding the enemy positions in dark shadows."

When Jim Rowe rushed back to the radio to contact the artillery unit to correct the placement of flares, he was hit with two enemy bullets in his right arm. The bullets impacted Jim so hard that he went sprawling down the side of the hill. With him he carried the microphone of the radio. The microphone had been shot away from its attachment to the radio. The radio was also destroyed, having absorbed more than 25 bullets.

Jim crawled toward the secondary radio, which Roger Smith had carried. He found Roger had been seriously wounded in the throat. The radio was also inoperable. Jim then located his M-14 rifle. He saw an enemy soldier in the shadows and fired; but didn't know if his shot hit his target.

At that moment Jim was hit again, a bullet striking his shoulder, just to the left of his neck. The bullet traveled through the back muscle just above the shoulder blade, pushed itself between the blade and spine, through the rib cage, perforating the left lung sack, which, upon deflating, collapsed his left lung. The bullet continued its journey, passing just to the left of his heart, underneath his diaphragm, destroyed his spleen, entered his stomach and finally came to rest in his intestines. This wound effectively put Jim Rowe out of action for the night.

Jim O'Leary went to Sgt. Starbuck's aid, dragging him back to within the relative security of the "V". He placed a bandage on the back of the sergeant's head and put the sergeant' s gas mask on to hold the bandage in place. O'Leary was then wounded and fell into a slit trench. Boo Boo Smith pulled O'Leary out of the trench.

Boo Boo Smith performed other heroic deeds. As Jim Rowe describes: "Roger 'Boo Boo' Smith, after being wounded along with the second radio, I swear he must have spent the remainder of that night keeping me from getting killed outright. After being shot three times and two subsequent grenade blasts throwing me down the slope towards the enemy positions, Smith crawled down the slope, in full view of the enemy, to retrieve me, half carrying and half dragging me back up the slope to something of a position of safety and was shot for his trouble. At another time during the darkness of the night, an enemy soldier, making a "Sweep" over the left wing and apparently thinking we were all dead, discovered me still alive. As I watched him raise his bayonet fixed rifle in anticipation of sending me to my death, 'Boo Boo' Smith shot and killed him instead with a burst of M-14 bullets."

Near dawn the hill became relatively quiet with the enemy only lobbing an occasional grenade or firing a burst of rifle fire into the Marine's position. Nevertheless, the enemy decided to mount another major assault on the Marine's position. At this time the Marines still had 22-25 CS gas grenades. As the enemy assaulted the hill, the team set off the grenades. Atmospheric conditions were such that the gas formed a cloud around the hill. The enemy soldiers, encountering the gas, gagged, vomited and withdrew.

With dawn, Air Observers arrived. They were trying to determine what had become of the team since radio contact with had been lost. David Verheyn, now the acting patrol leader, signaled the AO pilot with a "star cluster" flare. The pilot responds by flying over the team's position. Shortly after, CH-46 helicopters arrived. As the choppers approached, the enemy started firing at them. The helicopters didn't attempt landing initially. As they moved away from the hill, F-4 "Phantom" jets began a series of repeated attacks on the enemy positions. Before long, the Sea Knight helicopters are able to land on top of the hill to extract the team. All are extracted, dead wounded, and two of the Marines who escaped injury.

In this battle, Sgt. Starbuck, Cpl. Shafer, PFC Armitage, and PFC Edward Smith died. Roger Smith, James O'Leary,

James Rowe, David Verneyn and Charles Davis were all wounded. Only Ray Chaplin and Klaus Urbanick survived unscathed. For their actions on this patrol Sgt. Starbuck was awarded the Silver Star Medal, Lance Corporal Verheyn, the Navy Cross, Lance Corporal Rowe, the Bronze Star Medal, PFC O'Leary, the Bronze Star Medal, and Roger Smith the Bronze Star Medal. Surely this was a team of heroes.

CHAPTER 17 - Team *Dockleaf*

At 5 foot, 10 inches tall, Rick Noyes wasn't a big guy; but he loved sports. At Princeton High School in Cincinnati, Ohio he played football for four years and participated in gymnastics and track. His father, a sheet metal mechanic, had served in the Navy during World War II. When Rick made the decision to join the Marines, he also had a brother in the Navy and sister in the Marines. A high school teacher, however, provided the greatest incentive for Rick to enlist. Another classmate asked this teacher why the United States should be involved in Vietnam. The teacher responded by holding up a map of the world that indicated all the countries of the world where the communist governments enslaved the populations. One of these countries was Cuba, located only ninety miles from the coast of the United States. The teacher proposed that if we didn't fight to halt the spread of communism where we had the opportunity to do so, we might soon find it encroaching on our own country, perhaps with Cuban Communists taking over Florida.

The Marines allowed Rick to join on a delayed enlistment. This gave Rick the opportunity to work as a lifeguard during the summer after his graduation from high school. In October 1966, however, he reported for Boot Camp at San Diego, California. Following his basic training, he went through recon training and was assigned to a Marine recon unit in the United States. At that time, Recon Marines were required to become qualified in parachute jumping and scuba diving. He received orders to go to Fort. Benning, Georgia for parachute training. The casualty rate in Marine recon units in Vietnam was so high, however, that the Rick was asked if he would volunteer to go to Vietnam right away and skip the parachute training. Rick volunteered. After landing in Danang in July of 1967 he was sent straight to the 3rd Reconnaissance Battalion at Khe Sanh. By January 11, 1968, Lance Corporal Noyes had been on between 30 and 40 patrols.

On January 11, 1968, LCpl Rick Noyes was the point man for team *Dockleaf*. The team had been assigned the task of doing a reconnaissance of Hill 881N. Actually *Dockleaf* was substituting for another team that were originally assigned the mission. The leader of that team, however, had fallen in a trench and wrenched his knee.

Corporal Richard Healy was *Dockleaf's* team leader. Like Rick Noyes, Corporal Healy was a veteran of many patrols. He'd grown up in Toledo, Ohio. There Rich went to St. James Grade School and Central Catholic High School. He played football in high school and was a guard on the all-city second team.

Accompanying team *Dockleaf*, was 2ndLt Randall D. Yeary of Kingsport, Tennessee. Lt. Yeary had only recently arrived in Vietnam and was along to learn the particular details of conducting a patrol in the area. A Tennessee native, Randall Yeary spent his early years on a farm. He had an older sister and a younger brother. The brother, Linnis was six years younger; but liked to follow Randall wherever he went. Living in the country, they enjoyed pleasures like swinging on grapevines, swimming in a swimming hole created by damming a creek and having dogs and a pony. Randall was mischievous however, and managed to find unique ways to get into trouble. He attempted to ride a calf; but quickly learned the calf would have no part of it. Then there was the time he and a cousin were playing in the chicken house and found some blasting caps. They nearly scared themselves to death when they set one off. On another occasion, Randall came running to the house, announcing in a worried voice:

"I don't know what happened to the chicken."

His parents soon learned he had held it under water until it passed out.

In high school at Ketron High in Kingsport Tennessee, he played the position of guard on the football team. He also managed to get a partial scholarship to Eastern Tennessee University at Kingsport. Getting through college had its challenges. Randall married young and while in college soon had a daughter to support. To provide for his family, he worked at three part-time jobs. Nevertheless, he graduated with a degree in history. After graduating, Randall became a Marine Officer because he thought the Marine Corps would provide the best opportunities for himself and his family.

The first three days of patrol went without incident. The team had neither contact nor even sitings of the enemy. Then, on the 14th, as pointman, Richard Noyes moved over the crest of Hill 881N, he was showered by Chinese-Communist (Chi-com) hand grenades. Somehow, Noyes managed to kill both of the first two attackers, despite grenades exploding around him. Apparently Rick had unknowingly walked into an enemy position, right past two NVA soldiers who occupied previously dug fighting holes. One of the grenades pitched by these two bounced off Ken Martin; but shrapnel from the blast wounded Ken in the foot.

The team backed off the hill, retracing their steps, and forming the customary 360 degree defensive position. Rick Noyes had a LAAW (Light Anti-tank Assault Weapon). He asked Ken how to arm it. In the moment of confusion, which followed, the LAAW went off accidentally. Since a LAAW can be used only once (like a grenade), the team no longer had this weapon in their arsenal.

During the confusion of this initial contact with the NVA, Lt Yeary was shot. Corporal Healy struggled to get the Lieutenant back up the hill and into hasty defensive circle set up by the rest of team *Dockleaf*. The lieutenant had received four or five bullets in the thigh and upper groin. Corporal Healy, trying to help the Lieutenant, called to Ken Martin to provide covering fire into a nearby tree line. Ken obliges, but sees no apparent enemy presence there. Nevertheless, a RPG (rocket-propelled grenade) comes sailing from the tree line. It strikes Corporal Healy and explodes. The grenade immediately kills both Corporal Healy and Lieutenant Yeary. The blast from the grenade also threw Ken into the air. He then landed on his face in the dirt and is unconscious for a while.

When Ken Martin regained consciousness, he began groping on his hands and knees looking for his rifle, which disappeared during the blast from the RPG. By now enemy rounds are impacting all round him. To Ken's shock, he discovers one more thing, he can't hear! Spotting an old bomb crater, he rolls into it. Soon Ulis Murray joins Ken in the crater.

Since Ken carried the secondary radio on patrol, he started to work on getting it operational. By this time, all the team members except Santos were wounded. They all managed to crawl into the bomb crater. They were forced to leave the bodies of Lieutenant Yeary and Corporal Healy behind. Rick Noyes made an attempt to find the bodies but couldn't. Apparently the RPG blast had thrown the bodies of the two Marines somewhere in the brush downhill.

At this point neither Ken Martin nor Ulis Murray had a rifle. Ken was on the radio now trying get either an air strike to support them or an artillery fire mission. Apparently there were no aircraft available to support them and an artillery battery that was available wouldn't give the remnants of the team a fire mission because the team couldn't provide the battery with any grid coordinates. The artillery battery didn't want to risk dropping rounds on team *Dockleaf.*

After about 20 minutes, Rick Noyes and Santos Morales suggested they'd better try to get out of there. Rick led them out, circled around the hill, and found another ridge where they could be extracted by helicopter. By this time Ken Martin had been wounded in the head, arm, leg and foot and had a couple of surface wounds in the shoulder. When the extract helicopter finally arrived, the primary radioman accidentally discharged his rifle. This gave everyone a scare since they had managed to break free of their NVA pursuers, and they didn't want to give their position away again. As the helicopter lifted off with the team, Ken borrowed the pointman's M-14 and fired out a helicopter porthole, emptying the ammunition magazine in a fit of rage.

The helicopter dropped the team at a medical aid station. Ken Martin, after being treated, was put on light duty and returned to his unit where he remained through the siege of Khe Sanh, which followed.

CHAPTER 18 - Corporal Bryan and Team *Barkwood*

When January 18, 1968 arrived, Corporal Charles William Bryan had been in Vietnam for three and a half months. An event occurred that day, which would soon impact Corporal Bryan and his team *Barkwood*. Corporal Bryan was in 1st Squad, 1st Platoon, 3rd Reconnaissance Battalion, 3rd Marine Division. 3rd Recon was just one of many units assigned the responsibility of defending Khe Sanh Combat Base. The total contingent of Marines numbered about 5,000. Located in the northwest corner of South Vietnam, Khe Sanh was ideally situated for observing and conducting military operations against enemy forces trying to enter South Vietnam from North Vietnam or Laos. By January 1968, recon patrols were discovering an increase in the number of enemy in the rugged terrain surrounding Khe Sanh. Within the mountains and valleys surrounding the base, obscured by thick jungle vegetation, some 20,000 enemy troops were amassing for the purpose of seizing the combat base.

Bill Bryan grew up in McKinney, Texas, located northeast of Dallas. His dad worked in a cotton mill and his mother worked in the McKinney high school cafeteria. His one brother, Joe Bob, was three years older than Bill. When he was young Bill joined the Boy Scouts. A boyhood friend, Ronnie Foster, remembers:

"Bill was a Boy Scout in every way. He was truthful, reverent, and respectful of others. He loved hunting, fishing, camping and spent as much time as possible outdoors."

In high school Bill took a liking to football. He played center on the McKinney High School team and lettered two years. His other interest, like most guys in high school, was girls. Bill and Ronnie continued to be buddies throughout high school. When it came time to decide on what to do after high school graduation, real life books on military history like *The Green Berets*, *Guadalcanal Diary*, and *Battle Cry* influenced both. In March 1966, Ronnie turned 18 and had to register for the draft. A few days afterward, Ron enlisted in the Marine Corps, being allowed to delay reporting to boot camp until after high school graduation. He was issued an official identification card which he enjoyed flashing around the high school. This got some of the other boys, including Bill Bryan interested in the Marine Corps. Ron arranged for Marine Sergeant who had recruited him to give the boys a talk at his house. The Sergeant sold Bill Bryan on the Marine Corps also, and Bill enlisted with the promise he and Ronnie would be allowed to go through basic training together. They were to report for duty two weeks after high school graduation.

During the two weeks between graduation and boot camp, the two boys did a lot of goofing around. They hung out at a local drive-in and an all-night café, playing their favorite songs on the jukebox. They also cruised around in their cars. Ron had a 1957 Chevy and Bill a 1956 Ford. They'd drive through the newly mowed hayfields at night chasing rabbits, trying to keep them in the headlights. The rabbits, however, were too swift and managed to escape any harm.

On Monday, June 20, 1966, Bill and Ron boarded a train that would take them to the Marine Corp Recruit Depot at San Diego, California. Departing from Dallas, Texas the train rolled from through the Texas Panhandle, New Mexico, and Arizona before entering Southern California. The boys enjoyed some spectacular viewing as the train crossed the Rocky Mountains, the Continental Divide, and the Arizona desert. For the two boys the train trip was the last treat they would enjoy before they began the rigorous experience of Marine boot camp.

Bill Bryan and Ron Foster completed boot camp together as well as four weeks in the Infantry Training Regiment at Camp Pendleton. After that, the Marine Corps separated the two. Ron Foster went to Motor Transport Training School. Bill Bryan went to Basic Infantry Training School where he would emerge as a Marine rifleman. Bill and Ron happened to meet again while enjoying a weekend liberty at Camp Pendleton's San Onofre Beach Club. Ron learned Bill would soon be shipping out for recon school in Hawaii. The two young Marines spent much of the day trying to surf, nearly drowned, and finally gave up and went to the club for a drink. Since both were under 21, they had to settle for a chocolate shake instead. Afterward they said good-bye, and their paths would not cross again.

During his first leave, Bill returned to McKinney. There he started dating Deidra Simpson. Diedra was a year younger than Bill and still in high school. She was a leader in the Marquettes, the girl's drill team, and a member of the National Honor Society. Although she wore her hair rather shortly cropped, her angelic face bore a feminine image that would turn the head of any guy in town.

After recon school, Bill was assigned to 2nd Platoon, Charlie Company, 1st Battalion, 27th Marines. This unit was stationed in Hawaii. Bill spent most of his time training with the unit as they prepared for possible deployment to Vietnam. He did manage a bit or recreation. A Staff Sergeant Burlim taught Bill how to hunt boar with a knife. The boar attacked, and the Staff Sergeant waited until the boar was almost to him. Then the Sergeant side-stepped, sticking the knife in the boar. Bill provided back-up with a .44 Magnum pistol, just in case the sergeant missed killing the boar with the knife. Bill also caught a Hammerhead shark, but didn't provide the details in his letter to his friend, Ron.

Bill got orders for Vietnam several months later. He was allowed a 30-day leave prior to reporting for embarkation. He went home and married Diedra. They were married in the family home of Diedra's parents. Young Oil Company owner, Joe Bob Young, provided a ranch house in the country for the newlyweds to enjoy a honeymoon. Deidra was working part time for Mr. Young at the time. The 30 days of leave flew by and soon Bill was back at Camp Pendleton for some final training in preparation for Vietnam.

Bill arrived in Vietnam in October 1967, but it was several months before he arrived for duty with 3rd Reconnaissance Battalion at Khe Sanh. He immediately won the acceptance of the rest of his teammates. As teammate P. J. Pagano describes:

"Bryan was a Corporal when he was assigned to 1st Squad of 1st Platoon. He had come in from a grunt unit and everybody liked him from the start, which is unusual, as most guys had to prove themselves first. We seemed to have an abundance of corporals in the outfit at the time and at first he went out on patrols as just one of the guys. It was sort of on the job training for all the stuff they didn't teach in recon school back at Pendleton. I was very impressed with Cpl. Bryan. We were operating in jungle, and I mean real jungle, the kind of place where if the enemy didn't kill you, the jungle itself would. He was strong, had a good attitude, and was very good at his job. I think I went on three missions with him as primary radio operator and he just seemed a lot more mature than most of us. I thought he was older as he was married and all, and was very surprised to learn that we were about the same age."

On January 14, 1968, recon team *Dockleaf* got caught in a NVA ambush. This incident was to have grave consequences for team *Barkwood*. During *Barkwood's* encounter with the enemy, the team leader, Lt. Randall Yeary was killed. Also killed was Corporal Richard Healy, the team's radioman. Upon hearing that *Dockleaf* was in trouble, 3rd Platoon, India Company, 2nd Battalion, 26th Marine Regiment was ordered to assist the team. Lieutenant Tom Brindley, platoon commander, ordered his men to leave behind their helmets and flak jackets. Carrying only water, weapons, and ammunition, the infantry platoon hurried back to the site of the *Dockleaf's* ambush to assist *Dockleaf* and recover the two dead Marines.

They assisted the remaining members of the recon team and recovered the bodies of Lt. Yeary and Cpl. Healy. It wasn't until *Dockleaf* and Brindley's platoon had returned to Khe Sanh, that they discovered they hadn't recovered Cpl. Healy's radio and "shackle sheets". Shackle sheets contain the code used by recon radiomen to transmit sensitive information like the team's position over the radio. In enemy hands, both the radio and the shackle sheets could be deadly. The radio would allow the NVA to listen in on the Marine conversations and possibly trick Marines on patrol into an ambush. Possession of the code would make following the

Marine's activities even easier.

India Company's 1st Platoon, led by 2nd Lt. Harry F. "Rick" Fromme received the assignment to locate and recover the radio and code sheets. They left Hill 881S for Hill 881N and the site of the previous day's ambush. Approximately halfway to the site, the platoon got into a firefight with the NVA. One Marine was killed and two injured. The platoon was ordered to return to Hill 881S.

India Company requested permission to try again. This time the entire company would go out to conduct a "reconnaissance-in-force". The regimental commander wanted to leave a team behind on Hill 881N to conduct further reconnaissance so Corporal Bryan and team *Barkwood* were ordered to accompany India Company. A helicopter delivered the team to Hill 881S to join India Company on the evening of January 19th.

Before dawn the next morning, India Company, along with team *Barkwood*, moved off Hill 881S, headed for 881N. In addition to Cpl. Bryan, were Cpl. Lionel Guerra, assistant team leader; Lance Corporal Robert "PJ" Pagano, radioman, Lance Corporal Thomas Hollis, PFC Paul Beddoe, PFC Ron Parr, and one other PFC, on his first assignment who remains unidentified. The team carried enough food, water, and ammunition for four or five days in the bush. They would accompany India Company to Hill 881N, then drop out to search for the missing radio and shackle sheets. India Company had orders to return to Hill 881S by dark that evening. Team *Barkwood*; on the other hand, would stay on Hill 881N until the missing items were found, they exhausted their supplies, or made contact with the enemy.

The group moved through the early morning fog and elephant grass. The infantry unit was following a trail through the grass, moving along slowly. This made the *Barkwood* team members nervous as recon teams tried to move swiftly and stay off trails. About a thousand yards into the patrol, the 1st Platoon of India made heavy contact with a large number of NVA. The platoon suffered several casualties and took up defensive positions.

Corporal Bryan

Corporal Guerra

The platoon didn't have enough men to both hold its position and evacuate its casualties, so the 2nd Platoon under 2nd Lt. Michael Thomas, assisted by setting up a landing zone behind the 1st Platoon to evacuate the casualties. While this was going on, 3rd Platoon, located on the right flank also made contact and suffered casualties. Since *Barkwood* had been behind 3rd Platoon, Cpl. Barkwood immediately led his team to assist.

As Pagano describes:

> "We were walking in Elephant grass that was about five to six feet tall. Being in the rear of the grunts, I could see just their helmets above the grass, and I remember thinking how funny that looked, like a bunch of turtles floating along in a sea of grass. All of a sudden the sound of a heavy machine gun broke the silence. Seven shots. I remember it like it was two seconds ago, three shots, a pause, and then four. All those turtles slowly submerged and it was just grass again. I was so enthralled with that visual that I

Lance Corporal Robert "PJ" Pagano

suddenly thought to myself, 'get down, stupid'. I know at least one guy was killed.

"Bryan offered our support to the grunts, since they were now shorthanded because of casualties, and I got on the radio and called in the air support and artillery that was standing by for recon use. It was obvious that our mission was scrubbed; but we weren't returning to 881 South like we were supposed to. Since we were carrying so much more ammo than the grunts, Bill passed a helmet around and we filled it with grenades and passed it on to them. The lieutenant had us set up an LZ and Bryan and I called in choppers to pick up the dead and wounded. I saw some Marines crawling and dragging a man's body back to the rear. As we sat there in a small circle, two members of the grunt platoon crawled to a stop next to us. They were exhausted from dragging a tall red-haired Marine by his arms. His eyes were glazed and he had a battle dressing over his heart. As he was lying next to me, the lieutenant asked me to see if he was still alive. I couldn't find a pulse and couldn't detect any breathing, so I said, 'I think he's dead, sir.' The lieutenant told me to close his eyes, which I did. The chopper came into the LZ which we had set up just behind our little circle and the two Marines dragged their buddy off in that direction."

The 3rd Platoon commander ordered Corporal Bryan to clear one of two landing zones for the medevac helicopters to land. The first helicopter attempted to land at the LZ cleared by the 2nd platoon. It was shot down by enemy fire and crashed about 200 yards down the slope from 1st and 2nd Platoons. Members of those platoons spent a harrowing thirty minutes under heavy fire as they tried to reach the downed crew. They managed to rescue the crew with most of the crew members wounded but none killed. Team *Barkwood*, meanwhile had secured the second LZ and, crouching low in the elephant grass, fired grenades from M-79 grenade launchers at enemy positions. Corporal Guerra describes what happened next:

"A little bit later after we were re-joined by Bryan and Pagano, the word came down to fix bayonets and get ready to assault the hill. I was thinking that this was really crazy since we were recon and we didn't have helmets, flak jackets, or bayonets either for that matter. So we all just looked at each other and said, 'OK, let's go,' formed up on line, and started assaulting the hill."

Nevertheless, Team *Barkwood* was needed to replace the 3rd Squad of 3rd Platoon, as that squad had suffered so many casualties. As Pagano describes:

"The 3rd Platoon grunts had so many casualties that

we became their first squad, and the Lieutenant had us get on line for an assault against the dug-in NVA. It was just like in the old movies where they would walk on line, rifles fired from the hip, right into the flaming muzzles of the entrenched enemy. Then we got the word to fix bayonets. I'm thinking, what, are they crazy or something? Here I am armed to the teeth and they want me to stab somebody? I remember thinking, 'This is it. This is the real thing.' Recon guys usually don't do walking assaults. But without a second thought, we advanced up that hill under the direction of Cpl. Bryan who knew exactly what to do as he had been with an infantry unit, and that's what they do."

Guerra: "The assault began and we almost immediately came under heavy fire by an enemy position on higher ground. They were right there in front of us and I don't know exactly how long we fought them."

Pagano: "We were on the right side of the finger and with the grass so tall and thick, I couldn't see any grunts to my left. I figured there was a gap there and that wasn't good, so I moved to that position to fill in. Bryan reluctantly said OK, as he preferred the radioman be in a less conspicuous position. I was the left most person in our team as we started up the hill. Not being able to see the grunts, I didn't know if they were advancing or not. But we were. I could only see Lionel to my right, but I knew the rest of the team was to his right. Corporal Bryan directed that I stay slightly behind the line with him. Almost as soon as we started out, a hole opened between us and the infantry on the left. I shouted to Corporal Bryan that I was moving forward to plug the hole. The terrain and elephant grass soon caused us to lose contact with the infantry and each other. We all continued up the hill. I found myself to the left of Guerra and we went single file for a few feet until we were on top of the hill.

We stopped for a moment and an 81mm mortar round landed just in front of us. I was hit a second later and Lionel (Guerra) was hit a second after that (both by rifle fire). We were taking fire from the Marines at the bottom of the hill as well as from the NVA whom we were amongst (I was hit by a Marine bullet). I got on the air without much ceremony and said, 'Check fire. Check fire you're cutting us to pieces up here.' A few seconds later, Bryan called to me to stop the mortar and rifle fire from the friendlies. I told him I had done so and that I was hit. He said he knew I was hit as I had been yelling it (I guess I got a little upset for a second). He crawled over and while I was on the radio (now working choppers) he got up on his elbows to rip open a battle dressing for my wound. An NVA no farther than six feet away cranked a round at us that passed my left ear, over my chest, and into Bryan's armpit. I stopped transmitting after a while because my hands and face fell asleep and I became very tired. I had tied a tourniquet but had lost a great deal of blood and was still losing some."

The 3rd Platoon with Team *Barkwood* made it to the top of Hill 881 North; but the Platoon leader, Lieutenant Brindley and Corporal Bryan were killed in the process. Corporal Guerra describes Corporal Bryan's death as follows:

"He could see that Pagano and I, lying not more than six or seven feet apart, were in bad shape and needed to be medevacked as soon as possible or we were surely going to bleed to death. Before I knew what he was doing, Bryan jumped up to run to the aid of Pagano and to retrieve the radio. That was where he got hit, once by an AK-47 round. He died face down. His death came instantly."

The NVA who killed Cpl Bryan then tried to get Pagano and Guerra with a grenade. As Cpl Pagano describes:

"Lucky for me it was a Chi-Com grenade and they

had a reputation of blowing to one side instead of in all directions. It got me mostly in the hands and face, but not as bad as it could have. .... Somehow I managed to throw a grenade at the bastard. After it went off, I didn't hear anything from him again. I don't know if I killed him or scared him off. I couldn't much move at all by then, I was numb all over."

The team had now become separated from the rest of the platoon and all its members had been wounded. For the next couple of hours the members of India Company who hadn't been injured were busy locating the team members, evacuating the casualties and getting reorganized. As the Company Commander, Captain Dabney stated, "It was too late to proceed further, and the company had lost almost fifty Marines killed and wounded." Corporal Guerra describes being reunited with the company:

"I was lying there in the grass still trying to stop the bleeding, not sure if everybody was dead or what. The amount of fire going on all around us was still hot and heavy. A Marine sergeant, I didn't know him but will never forget him, crawled up from out of nowhere, tapped me on the shoulder, and said he was going to get us out of there. He checked on Bryan first. I had lost a lot of blood and was probably in shock from the grenade concussion. I asked him how Bryan was and he said, 'He's dead.' I then said 'How about him?, meaning Pagano. The sergeant said he's OK and that he would come right back for him. He helped me crawl away and I tried to follow him the best that I could. My arm was really in bad shape. I thought for sure that I was going to lose it. When we reached what we thought was the safety of the company, not far away at all, maybe twenty feet, the sergeant headed back. Just then we started getting shot at again from behind us as well as in front. I heard a familiar thud and the guy right beside me got hit in the leg. We were getting hit from all sides again, and apart from being messed up pretty bad, I didn't have my glasses or my weapon. There wasn't much I could do at the time, and I remember saying a prayer and making the sign of the cross. It seemed like all of a sudden this great feeling of serenity came over me."

Shortly after, Guerra was medevacked. He describes the experience as follows:

"Finally somebody said medevac was coming in. I was so mad that I got up and walked to the chopper even though we were still under heavy fire. I was not only sad, but I was mad too. I was mad because I didn't know what had happened to the rest of the team, and nobody could tell me. The chopper took us back to Khe Sanh. The floor was slick with blood from the other dead and wounded Marines on board. When we got there many of the members of 3rd Recon were there to meet us. That was something that Recon always did when we had wounded. Always, always, always, they met the returning teams. Somebody offered me a cigarette and I took it and then said, 'Wait a minute. I don't smoke.' I was still mad because somebody asked me where my friend Cpl. Charles Bryan was, and I had to tell him that he was dead I was mad at the whole situation, was especially about my arm, and mad at myself because I thought maybe I could have done something different to save his life. Once we got back to Danang, a hospital bus met the plane on the runway. It was set up for stacking stretchers on racks, and on the way to the hospital I heard someone saying, 'I'm gonna die. I'm gonna die.' I couldn't see him, but recognized the voice. It was my buddy Paul Beddoe from Barkwood. I got mad at him and told him he wasn't going to die. He died the next day."

Pagano was still on the hill when the helicopter took Guerra away. He describes what happened to him:

"After a while I didn't have the strength in my hands to key the handset. I could hear people on the radio trying to reach us, but I couldn't do anything about it. As I lay flat on my back looking up at the sky with the body of Bill Bryan still stretched across my legs, I watched a little black speck become larger and larger until I could tell it was a plane. It was a Marine fighter jet, an F4 Phantom, and was coming directly at me. Having experienced close air support many times I knew what he was doing. He came in for a dummy run, zooming by right above me, low enough that I could count the rivets on the fuselage and feel the heat from his engine. And then he circled for the real thing. I didn't know what his mission was, bombs, or napalm. I could see the snake eyes (two hundred and fifty pound bombs) on his wing. I was praying it wasn't napalm, because I was sure that he didn't know I was there and was about to blow the hell out of that hillside, which was still crawling with NVA. I really didn't want to die from napalm. I had first-hand knowledge of what it did from doing bomb-damage assessments. That was when my worst nightmare was becoming reality. I saw the two napalm canisters as they dropped from under the wings and come tumbling through the air toward me. I closed my eyes, took a deep breath, and covered my face and accepted my fate. Luckily they hit just over the crest of the hill, but I really felt the heat. And then I heard two chopper pilots talking to each other."

"Have you been monitoring Barkwood?" inquired one pilot.

"Yes, that was a sad situation," the other responded. Pagano: "They were talking about us in past tense. They thought we were dead. Hell, I wasn't dead yet and had to somehow let them know. From where I was, I couldn't see anybody but NVA soldiers. I figured I was probably the only American still alive on that hill. I didn't know what had happened to everybody. I managed to get the handset under my head close to my mouth, and could key it by pressing my head down. I was calling for anybody who could hear me. 'All stations this net. This is Barkwood. Be advised this station is still up.' There was an embarrassed silence for a few minutes, and then a voice came back:

'Barkwood, this is India Six Actual, (Captain Dabney) I've got six Marines here who have volunteered to come up and get you. You up for it?'

I answered, 'That's affirmative.'

They didn't know exactly where I was, so we set up a signal. He said they would stay on my frequency and ask for two quick shots from time to time to locate me. It was pretty risky since we were still under a lot of fire and I knew the NVA were all around and my rescuers had to crawl. It was very hard for me to fire my weapon because of the condition of my hands. We signaled back and forth three times. On the third time, the bolt of my M16 locked open and gray smoke circled up and out. I was out of rounds. In the condition I was in there was no way that I could retrieve another magazine and insert it. I didn't know how they would find me now. It had started to rain, and big huge raindrops were hitting me in the face. I was afraid to look at my watch and see what time it was. I was dreading the dark. I knew that if they didn't find me before then, I was dead. Suddenly this dirty, grimy, goofy-looking head sticks out of the grass just a few inches from my face.

"'Are you *Barkwood*?' he asked just as casually as if we were meeting on a street corner in Manhattan. I was never so happy in my life. With him was Ron Parr, from team *Barkwood*. He was wounded but had that big grin on his face that he always had. At the time we had to leave Bill's body as there was no way they could retrieve both of us. The NVA knew we were close, but I don't think they realized just how close we were. They could have killed us all easily. Those guys got me down the hill, dragging me by my belt suspenders a few inches at a time, under fire all the way, where I was loaded onto a Medevac chopper, flew out still under heavy fire, and never saw any of my teammates again."

This was the end of the war for both Guerra and Pagano. Both were wounded so badly that recovery would take a long time. However, both are still alive at the time this book is being written. Captain Dabney describes what happened after the recovery of the surviving members of team *Barkwood*:

"With some difficulty and a few more casualties, we were back on 881 South shortly after dark, with all hands, including the recon team, accounted for, either by nose count or by medevac records. All outlying positions in the Khe Sahn area were attacked that night except Hill 881 South. I believe we were not attacked because we had pre-empted the attacking force and had hurt it enough to spoil its plans, or at least found and fixed it so that we could pour on the supporting arms, which we did throughout the night.

The recon team was critical to the success of the recon-in-force. Without its voluntary attachment to 3rd Platoon, I'm not certain the assault would have succeeded. I also felt that the discipline of the team when it got separated during the assault was superb. All hands were hit, yet they stayed together, protected those who were too badly hurt to protect themselves, and repelled NVA counter-attacks as a team, until India's Marines could find and help them.

I regret that I don't know the team members, but the team was only with us for a few hours before every man was Medevacked. In a perfect world, we'd have tracked all hands down, gotten statements for award recommendations and passed our thanks and compliments on to 3rd Recon Battalion about the team's awesome performance under fire. But it is not a perfect world. The siege of Khe Sahn began with first light the next morning, and by noon, India had lost another twenty KIA or WIA to NVA artillery, as well as having a Medevac helo shot down. So it went for the next three months, and by the time it was over, there were few left in India, or, I suspect, in Recon, who could accurately recount the events of 20 January, 1968. That day became like so many that followed it, a blur of chaotic fire-fights, watchful waiting in the night and fog, and finally, triumph.

After we returned to 881 South, I recommended to my battalion commander that the team leader, Cpl. Bryan, be put in for the Navy Cross. At that time, I did not know whether he'd made it or not, but I felt that his action in volunteering the team as an assault element, the spirit and effectiveness with which the team carried out the assault, and the superb discipline and cohesiveness of the team after it was hit, were the epitome of the Marine spirit and evidence of his outstanding and selfless leadership under fire."

Corporal Bryan did receive the Navy Cross posthumously. The award was presented to his wife, Deidra. Out of the seven members of the Bravo Company, 3rd Recon team, two died from wounds received that day on Hill 881 North, Cpl. Charles William Bryan and PFC Paul Beddoe. Tom Hollis was wounded but returned to duty. He was killed eight days later during the seventy-seven day siege of the Khe Sanh Combat Base, by a direct hit on his position during a rocket attack. Ron Parr was wounded, and died in 1996 or 1997 due to an aneurysm. As noted above, Guerra and Pagano were hospitalized and saw no further action. The seventh member was on his first patrol; but no one living remembers who he was or what eventually became of him.

CHAPTER 19 - *Dallas Girl*

It was April 4, 1968 and the Marines at Camp Carroll were getting tired of being pounded by enemy mortar rounds. As a new mortar assault ensued, team *Dallas Girl* was going to do something about it. They were out to find the NVA observation post that was directing the enemy mortar fire.

Eight Marines and a Navy Corpsman formed the team *Dallas Girl*. The highest ranking of these was Second Lieutenant Donald John Matocha.

Lieutenant Matocha's home was Smithville, Texas. He was the oldest child in the family of nine children. As such, he knew he should set a good example for his brothers and sisters. His father, Raymond Matocha, of Czechoslovakian ancestry and mother, Celestine Goertz Matocha, of German ancestry raised the family on a farm near Smithville. The house had only one bathroom, so sharing it was a major

Lieutenant Matocha

problem. The Matocha family raised all their own food including livestock and a 2-acre vegetable garden. All the children participated in raising the crops, working the fields, and only breaking in the middle of the day for a big family meal and brief respite from the hot Texas sun.

As the son of good Catholic parents, Donald became an altar boy at the church the family attended. His parents would lead the family in saying the rosary every night. On nights when the parents weren't at home, Donald would take charge of this task. Of course he wasn't always the exemplary older brother. He encouraged his younger sister, Loretta to smoke grapevine when she was five. He also got in trouble for seeing how many pecans he could get to land on a neighbor's roof. Then there was the time he saved up some money and bought a large box of fireworks. His mother disapproved at the extravagance of spending money on something destined to go up in smoke.

Donald also had a special interest in baseball. He would listen to baseball games on the radio during the families' midday break from work, and he loved to collect baseball cards. When it came time to attend high school, he went to Smithville High. There he played football, ran track and was a member of Future Farmers of America. He also excelled academically and, upon graduation, was accepted for admission to Texas A & M University. Donald obtained money for college by the sale of livestock which he raised. At Texas A & M, Donald Matocha studied civil engineering and completed requirements for the degree in only three and a half years, graduating with honors. An outgoing young man, Donald assisted other classmates who were having trouble with the tough courses. Donald was the first Matocha to attend college. He was a member of the Corps of Cadets at A & M and went on to become an Officer of Marines.

Providing medical assistance for the team was Stan "Doc" Sellers. Another native Texan, Doc attended high school in Bandera, Texas. He went out for football; but had to quit after he collided with a goal post during a practice session. The resulting concussion meant a high risk of death if he should ever sustain a severe blow to the head again. When Doc Sellers graduated from high school, more and more men were being drafted into the Army to serve in Vietnam. When Doc Sellers went to the local courthouse to check on his draft status, he discovered he was "number 1" on the list. Since his father had been a pharmacist mate in the Navy, Stan Sellers decided to join the Navy. The Navy made him a Corpsman, so soon it was off to Vietnam for duty with a Marine unit.

Arriving in Danang, Republic of Vietnam, with a group of other Navy Corpsman, Stan had two choices, infantry or recon. The official in charge of assigning the newly arrived Corpsmen told them their "life expectancy" with the grunts (infantry) was 30 seconds and with recon was 90 seconds. Stan opted for the longer life expectancy and volunteered for recon. He was soon whisked away to the north of South Vietnam to become a member of the 3rd Reconnaissance Battalion.

Doc Sellers first patrol occurred in December, 1967. On this patrol, the team he was with sighted a NVA patrol in a little ravine without the NVA being aware if the presence of the recon team. One of the members of the team carried an M-60 machine gun, another had an M-79 grenade launched. These two team members opened up on the enemy and killed all the enemy patrol. The Marine recon team was able to capture weapons and papers from the NVA, which entitled the Marine recon team to a recreational visit to China Beach. China Beach was located near Danang in the Republic of Vietnam. The breezy expanse of sandy oceanfront provided a welcome relief from the jungle, elephant grass or rice paddies where the war was waged. If the sharks weren't active off the coast, it was a good place to swim also. Salt water can do wonders for a body used to being soaked in body sweat.

Later that month, Doc Sellers experienced a rather weird situation. While patrolling in Quang Tri province, the team he was on spotted an NVA patrol. Following standing operating procedures, the team backed off, and, after dark, settled into their 360-degree defensive perimeter for the night. Later, an NVA patrol approached and the team held their breath as the NVA walked right through the team's area without spotting any of the Marines.

Andre Boersma was the primary radioman for *Dallas Girl*. Andre emigrated from Holland. His parents settled in Minneapolis, Minnesota. Here he attended North High were he sampled both wrestling and gymnastics. He settled on gymnastics. He graduated from North High in 1966. Five of his high school buddies talked him into joining the Marine Corps with them. They attended boot camp together. After completion of boot camp and Infantry Training Regiment, Andre was sent to radio school where he became qualified as a Marine radioman. His initial assignment was to the 1st Battalion, 3rd Marine Regiment; but while being conveyed by a ship from Okinawa to Vietnam, he joined a Recon unit onboard.

Michael Kornezos grew up in Minnesota too. His home was in the community of Cass Lake. Here he grew up in country noted for its fish and game. As a result, Michael developed a love of fishing and hunting. He attended Cass Lake High School where he played both basketball and baseball. Basketball was his favorite.

While visiting with his girlfriend one day, her brother showed Michael the book, similar to a high school yearbook that recorded significant events during the brother's platoon's progress in Marine Corps Boot Camp. This was incentive enough for Michael to join and he was soon off to the Marine Corps Recruit Depot in San Diego.

When Michael completed all the basic training, he was assigned to 1st Battalion, 3rd Marine Regiment, then to a recon unit while on the ship in transit to Vietnam. Arriving in the late summer of 1967, by April 1968 he was a seasoned veteran and in the position to lead a patrol of his own.

The other member of this patrol for whom a little more is known than the bare minimum facts was Mike Cappa. Mike attended Balboa High School in San Francisco, California, graduating in 1965. His favorite sport was baseball. When Mike graduated, the draft was looming, so with some friends, he enlisted in the Marine Corps. Later, at Camp Pendleton, California, Mike volunteered for recon. On this mission with team *Dallas Girl* he was "Tail End Charlie". The last in the line as the team moved through the bush, Mike's responsibility was to see that the enemy didn't sneak up on them from behind.

Other members of the team include Gary Myers, Leslie Goebel, and Nickie Smith whose pre-Marine days must remain an unknown for the time being.

On 4 April 1968, team *Dallas Girl* left Camp Carroll, on foot, heading toward Dong Ma Mountain, seeking to find the NVA forward observers who were directing the artillery and mortar bombardment of Camp Carroll. As Doc Sellers describes:

> "The artillery and mortar tube had been shelling Highway 9 and Camp Carroll with pinpoint accuracy because of the NVA OP position on the south side of Dong Ma Mountain. There were several skeletons of supply trucks laying on the side of Highway 9. We passed them at the beginning of our patrol." About halfway up the mountain, the team discovered a communications wire and decided to follow it. They expected contact with the NVA at any time; but saw no one. As darkness neared, the members of *Dallas Girl* formed a 360-degree perimeter and placed claymore mines on the perimeter as a defense against unwelcome guests that night. Although the team settled down with nervous expectation of an impending attack, none came.

At 6:00 a.m. the morning of April 5th, the team was on the move again. As the team advanced up the ridgeline, they observed more and more signs that the enemy had been there. They found a 2-foot wide trail running northwest to southwest up toward the top of the hill and an enemy communications wire. The communications wire running next to the trail was spliced in several places. Team *Dallas Girl* also spotted a portion of an 82mm enemy mortar tube. The team estimated the tube had been destroyed within the past 2 days. They also passed 3 two-man fighting holes.

Arriving on the crest of the ridge, the team spotted a

formation of rocks. As the patrol members approached these rocks, the point man heard voices coming from the rocks. Now it appeared there might be an enemy bunker built into the rocks. Team *Dallas Girl* formed a defensive perimeter stance as Lt. Matocha advanced to the suspected enemy bunker. Lt. Matocha threw a CS gas grenade into the rock formation. Then, as Doc Sellers describes:

"It all happened so fast. About the same time Lt. Matocha threw a CS grenade unto the cave where the NVA were, I fired at an enemy in the site of my weapon. All the sudden it seemed like the whole world had exploded into one big firefight. The NVA regulars were firing from what seemed like every piece of rock and bush of landscape that was there."

Team *Dallas Girl* dashed for a nearby bomb crater and set up their 360-degree defense. Then Doc Sellers saw Lt. Matocha get hit. The lieutenant succumbed to a full burst from an enemy AK-47. Doc started toward Lt. Matocha; but, just 10 feet short, an enemy round pierced Doc's leg and he fell to the ground. By now other Marines were hit.

Doc Sellers struggled to reach Lt. Matocha. Fierce automatic fire from the enemy prevented him from advancing. The Doc was only about five from the lieutenant at this point. The lieutenant was clearly dead and the Corpsman could do no more for him. Meanwhile the wounded; but living among the rest of his team needed him. He moved toward the bomb crater where they had taken refuge. As Doc Sellers describes:

"There were two other Marines wounded. I moved towards where the radioman was. He had taken cover in some rocks at the north at the north side of the crater. He kept hollering that he could not feel his legs. The radioman had taken a round across his back criss-crossing his spine. Just as I pulled myself towards him I felt weak and dizzy. I fell backwards and passed out.

I came to a few minutes later. The assistant patrol leader was yelling "Corpsman up". I tried to get up again and move towards him (the assistant patrol leader). I started seeing black again. In a last ditch effort I threw my unit one bag (medical bag) towards him."

As team *Dallas Girl* battled approximately 15 NVA from the bomb crater, an air observer plane and helicopter gunships arrived and began strafing the enemy. CH-46 helicopters followed to extract the team. Using a hoist, the Doc Sellers and the three wounded Marines were lifted aboard the helicopter first. Gary Meyers, Michael Kornezos (now the acting patrol leader), and Nickie Smith were the last to board the helicopters. It was impossible to recover the body of Lt. Matocha.

The helicopters flew the team to Dong Ha Battalion Aid Station. Here the wounded men receive first aid treatment of their wounds. Andre Boersma was then flown to Guam for surgery. Afterwards he was sent to the Great Lakes Naval Center near Chicago for physical rehabilitation. Doc Sellers badly wounded in the legs, also required extensive medical treatment and physical rehabilitation. His legs would never be the same again. What happened to Mike Cappa and Leslie Goebel after being treated at the Battalion Aid Station is not readily known.

Nickie Smith was wounded the following day while serving on a reaction force attempting to recover the body of Lt. Matocha. On May 13, 1968, Lt. Bruce Wilson led a patrol back to the area where *Dallas Girl* made contact. This team ran into the NVA again. Gary Meyers, walking point, was killed. Eventually efforts to recover Lt. Matocha's body had to be called off. Thirty-six years later, however, in September 2004, the remains of Lt. Matocha were found and returned to Smithville, Texas for burial.

CHAPTER 20 - Hill 200

The stars fascinated Ted Whitlock. Living in North Las Vegas, Nevada, he had the opportunity to see both kinds, those visible in the desert sky and those performing in the casinos of Las Vegas. He would talk to his sister for hours on the universe and constellations.

As a boy he enjoyed the company of a dog named Buffy, a cat named Bootsy, and, of course, a sister, Donna. At age 10 he composed the following poem:

Why can't people learn to give,
To lend a hand to those in need?
That would be beautiful to me, INDEED.

While attending Rancho High School in North Las Vegas, Ted participated in music, football and swimming. He also liked to water ski and go to the mountains to camp out. Of course he had girlfriends also, Debbie was his favorite. Debbie had to move back east with her family, but Ted never lost his affection for her. As his sister describes, "He was one of the few guys I ever knew that actually liked to dance." One of Ted's favorite songs was *Eve of Destruction* by Barry Saddler. Buffy (the dog) destroyed the 45-rpm record containing the song, however. Ted also liked western movies starring Clint Eastwood. The Everly Brothers (a singing duo) were another favorite of Ted's. His sister, Donna also describes his encounter with a Las Vegas star:

"Ted was a bus boy at the Aladdin Hotel, just prior to joining the Marines. He worked the graveyard shift (probably meaning after midnight till 8 in the morning). One night, as he was on break, he saw this familiar looking fellow playing dollar slots (A slot machine is a form of gambling. In this case a person puts a coin in the machine, and, if lucky, the machine will spew back a bunch of coins. Otherwise, the player loses the coin. At the time Ted Whitlock was working at the Aladdin, a dollar was worth much more than today, so the player he observed had to have had a lot of money.) This guy had a rolling table stacked with silver dollars and was going from slot to slot. Ted recognized him and, although he was a fan, he just decided to treat him like a regular guy. He (Ted) made of some joke about the stack of dollars and they struck up a conversation. They talked about cars and Vegas, and Ted mentioned he was on break. Elvis (the man playing the slot machines) offered to buy him coffee. So they had coffee, and, as Ted's break was over, he turned to Elvis and said: 'Well if you are not going to ask me for my autograph, how about giving me yours? It's for my sister.' Elvis says, 'Sure, for your SISTER, huh?' Ted assured him that he did have a sister who had his pictures all over her room.

That morning when he came home from work, he gave me the autograph written on an Aladdin Hotel napkin, but not before he said: 'Guess who bought me coffee last night?'

The next morning he came home and informed me that he (Ted) had bought Elvis coffee on his break. This went on for about a week. They just talked about regular guy stuff, but during those conversations, he told Elvis that he had joined the Marines, and was leaving for boot camp very shortly. Elvis wondered if there was anything he could do for him. He (Ted) said yes, he would like it if he could bring his girlfriend to the hotel to meet him. Elvis said, "I'll do better than that." He (Elvis) told him (Ted) to bring her to the restaurant at a certain time and they would be seated in the appropriate place. When Ted and his girlfriend (Louise) arrived, they were seated in a large booth. Louise was seated in a position that would not let her see who was sitting behind her. Then, Elvis, seated with all of his buddies, stands up in the restaurant and says: 'Hey fellows, look who is here, it's Ted Whitlock, maybe we can get him to join us.' Louise turns around and is face to face with Elvis Presley (the real one). Elvis bought them a lovely dinner and wished Ted well, and told him to look him up when he got out of the Marines. Well, Elvis didn't give him a car, like he did for so many others, so often, but those people never got to eat with him. Ted considered him a friend after that."

Why did Ted Whitlock join the Marines? Perhaps it was his desire to help others. He read the book written by Dr. Tom Dooley, describing the atrocities committed by the Communist in Southeast Asia. He also harbored a desire to be a policeman. Ted learned that prior service as a Marine increased his chances of being accepted into the Las Vegas Police Department. He certainly didn't have a predisposition to violence. He chose to be a Recon Marine because, as he told his sister: "If I ever have to kill anyone, it had better be because it is simply him or me. I couldn't just shoot at someone from afar and forget that he is still a human being."

Ted arrived in Vietnam June 27, 1968. He became a member of Echo Company (Company E), 1st Reconnaissance Battalion. There he soon became a member of team *Flakey Snow* led by Corporal Roger Keister.

PFC Ted Whitlock

By June 1968, Corporal Roger Keister was a seasoned veteran of the Vietnam War. After graduating from Central High School in Phoenix, Arizona in 1964, he decided to join the Marine Corps to test himself. Being an intelligent lad, the Marine Corps wanted Roger to enter in a technical specialty. Then Private Kiester insisted that he wanted to be in the infantry. As the demand for grunts (infantrymen) in Vietnam was increasing almost daily at the time, the Marine Corps granted his request. After infantry training, Roger Kiester volunteered for recon.

On June 8, 1966, Roger Kiester arrived in Vietnam to begin his first tour of duty there. From his arrival until his departure on August 31, 1967, he participated in 53 long - range reconnaissance patrols. After his return to the United States, Roger Keister left the Marines for a time; but returned

March 6, 1968. By April 12, 1968 he was back in Vietnam. This time he was assigned to Echo Company, 1st Reconnaissance Battalion. In late July he was assigned to be the patrol leader of a nine-man squad of recon Marines.

One of Echo Company's responsibilities was to occupy and protect an observation post located on Hill 200. Observation posts such as this were located (usually on a hilltop) where the occupants could observe enemy operations below. When VC or NVA soldiers were spotted, the team leader would radio to an artillery battery for a fire mission on the enemy. Normally being assigned to an observation post provided a rest for Recon Marines. They got to stay in one place instead of patrolling through jungle. This was especially important in August when the temperature regularly reached 120 degrees Fahrenheit during the day.

The observation post was not well fortified. For protection against incoming rounds the Marines constructed bunkers. They were part below ground and part above ground. First the Marines would dig a "fighting hole" in the ground. Around the fighting hole they placed sandbags. Then, with lumber flown in by helicopter they would build a roof over the hole. The roof was then covered with sandbags. This left only a minimum amount of open space or aperture between the roof and sandbags in front of the bunker. From this aperture the Marines could fire on attacking enemy forces. More importantly the restricted open space made it difficult for the enemy to lob grenades into the bunker, and the sandbags on the roof would absorb shrapnel from grenades landing there. To retard the enemy from charging the bunkers, the Marines surrounded the perimeter of the observation post with barbed wire and concertina wire (wire made with little barbed projections like small razor blades). They also placed claymore mines around the perimeter. Besides their personal M-16 rifles, observation posts were often equipped with one or more machine guns and mortar tubes.

When Corporal Keister got the order to man Hill 200, he asked around and learned the hill had a large perimeter. He felt his nine-man squad wasn't enough to defend it during an attack. He asked the Company Commander for an additional squad. He was told that, of the 35 squads in the battalion, his was the only one available to relieve the men currently occupying the hill, who were needed for another mission. He was also told his mission was only to observe the valley below and not much was going on out there and therefore, he would need only one squad.

Nevertheless, he also learned that enemy forces had probed the hill a couple of times in the past few weeks. Still none of his superiors seemed concerned. He asked if he could take some of the non-essential personnel from the company up with him. He was granted permission and managed to get eight volunteers from among company clerks, men assigned to work parties, etc. A couple of them even had previous field experience.

Arriving on Hill 200, Corporal Keister had a short time to talk to the patrol leader he was replacing. The patrol leader claimed that one of his men, Corporal Evans had gotten nervous the previous night and fired off a couple of hundred rounds of machine gun ammunition the previous night; but the other Marines on the hill thought it was just his (Evans') imagination.

Corporal Keister talked to Cpl. Evans privately. Evans told Keister, "These guys can go to hell because somebody was out there."

Then Evans pointed out exactly where he had heard the noise. Afterwards, the outgoing patrol was flown out and the remainder of Keister's patrol landed. Keister inspected the defenses. In his words:

"By my standards, the place was a disaster area. The bunkers were just foxholes with a few sand bags around them. The defensive wire was in bad shape and there was not nearly enough of it. In places, you could easily step over it. Most of my troops had been here before. They thought it was all as it should be and there was nothing to worry about. I suggested to these people that they do some improvements on the bunkers and they literally didn't know what I was talking about. I decided to show them by example. I put myself on the most likely avenue of approach, overlooking the position where Corporal Evans said he had heard movement, and started to rebuild the bunker there.

Right before dark, I took a couple of people down to where Corporal Evans said he had heard movement. About 15 meters in front of the wire, Lance Corporal Derenick, the squad's new radioman, found a crude knife. It was then I believed Corporal Evans' story about somebody being down there. We went back up the hill and I sent a message to the battalion about the knife and I directed them to send a copy to Corporal Evans. He had taken enough crap about shooting at an imaginary Viet Cong.

By the end of the second day we had finished rebuilding the bunker. It looked pretty good. I informed everybody this was what I meant by a bunker and the next day I would began supervising them to build ones like it."

Accompanying Corporal Keister in the newly reconstructed bunker were Corpsman Ploetz, LCpl. Derenick, and PFC Scott Smith.

"Doc" Ploetz, the corpsman for the team, wasn't even an American citizen when he occupied the hill with team *Flakey Snow*. Norbert H. Ploetz was the son of a German immigrant. His father had been a pilot in the Luftwaffe during World War II. After WWII, Norbert's father moved to

Ontario, Canada where he worked as a pipe organ builder. Then Norbert's father got a job offer in Cleveland, Ohio, so he moved the family there.

Norbert attended West Tech High School in Cleveland. There he studied the design arts of drafting and architectural drafting in a special program sponsored by General Motors Corporation. He also pursued his interests in gymnastics and art. Graduating in 1966, Norbert joined the Navy, hoping to get additional technical training. The Navy, however, decided to make him a Medical Corpsman, Norbert's last choice of desired specialty training. After training at the Great Lakes Naval Facility near Chicago, he was sent to Camp Pendleton to train with the Marines. Norbert chose recon on his father's advice. His father convinced Norbert that his best chances of surviving in war would be with an elite group.

At Camp Pendleton, HM3 Ploetz sought to get naturalized as a citizen. After all, he had to sign an "Intent to Defend" the United States in order to enlist in the Navy and he was about to be sent to Vietnam where he might have to give his life defending the United States. The legal office at Camp Pendleton, however gave him no help. Instead they gave him some legal mumbo jumbo about having to apply for citizenship through the State of Ohio. This left a very bitter taste in the young Corpsman's mouth. When *Flakey Snow* landed on Hill 200, HM3 Ploetz had completed five long-range reconnaissance patrols.

At 4:00 a.m., August 1, 1968, HM3 Ploetz was taking his turn at watch next to the bunker reconstructed by Corporal Keister. Cpl Keister had just completed making the rounds of checking the other Marines standing watch on the observation post. He was going to get a little sleep. The evening before PFC Smith had accidentally punctured Cpl Keister's air mattress. With the ground inside the bunker being hard, the corporal decided to sleep on top of the bunker. As he lay on top of the bunker, still awaiting to fall asleep, HM3 Ploetz made a routine situation report to the 1st Reconnaissance Battalion Headquarters. Shortly after he reported, "All's Well", the VC struck.

HM3 Ploetz thought he saw what he thought was another Marine throw a lighted cigarette into the bunker Cpl Keister was laying on. It actually was an enemy satchel charge, which exploded, sending Cpl Keister flying into the air. As he recalls:

"Before I even hit the ground, I knew this was going to be the real thing. It took a second or two for me to get my act together. I started to run back up the hill. Most of the firing was from the enemy as most of my troops, did not have a clue as to what to do. I tripped over some sand bags and fell on top of my rifle, which had been lying next to me on the bunker. This I considered a major piece of luck, one of the many that I would encounter over the next hour. I got up, with my rifle in hand, and jumped into the hole where my new bunker had been. At the same moment, LCpl Derenick was busy changing magazines, which was the reason he did not have a chance to shoot me by mistake. He was happy about that and expressed his joy I was still alive, a thought he had not considered possible. His boot, along with a couple of his toes, had been blown off by the satchel charge, but this did not seem to slow him down much.

The radio, inside what was left of my bunker, could not even be found. My first obligation was to tell battalion we were in it and that we would need help. I left L.Cpl. Derenick in charge of the three men in this position and moved over to the other radio. When I got there, Sergeant Poppa (another radioman) had already gotten off a message to battalion and I thought they were on top of things, so I went off to another bunker where I had heard a lot of firing. By the time I got there, only one man, LCpl Jones, was still in the bunker and he was hurt too bad to save.

I started to head for the next bunker, to get somebody to man this position, when a satchel charge went off behind me and blew me into what I think was the remains of the ammo bunker."

At this time Cpl Keister was stunned by the explosion from the satchel charge and cannot be sure of what happened next. Nevertheless, his description of the action continues:

"Anyway, the next thing I remember was, this little guy with an AK-47 was standing almost on top of me and fired a short three or four round burst right at my face. He missed me and I rolled over out of his way and he fired another burst at me. Again, I tried to roll out of his line of fire and before I could bring my weapon to bear, he fired again. It was very dark that night. I was flipping around, in and behind, a big pile of sand bags. Even though he was close, I don't think the enemy soldier could really see me until he fired. Then, the light of his muzzle flashes would make me visible to him and he would re-aim his weapon and shoot again. My body movement could best be explained by observing a fish out of water, just flipping around at random. By the time he pointed at where he last saw me, I was no longer there. We went through what must have been six or seven of these little exchanges. He started to move back to change magazines and I got a chance to return the compliment, so to speak. Unlike me, who was hiding in the sand bags, he was silhouetted against the night sky. I did not miss him."

L.Cpl. Derenick located Cpl. Keister while Derenick was searching for grenades. A satchel charge had separated Derenick from his rifle and he was looking for a means to fight back. L.Cpl. Derenick threw the grenades into the bunker he had previously occupied, killing the VC who now Occupied it. He also managed to recover a rifle (his or one of the enemy's is not clear).

Then Cpl. Keister came upon L.Cpl. Irby outside the bunker he had formerly occupied with L.Cpl. Jones. Both of Irby's legs were mangled by high explosives. Cpl. Keister hid him in a ditch, covered him with a poncho and some sand bags and told him to play dead.

Next L.Cpl. Derenick started to yell for help. Keister ran over to him and discovered a grenade had exploded right next to his upper thigh, blown a big hole in his leg and removed a couple of inches of bone. As Cpl. Keister tried to drag Derenick to a safer spot, fragmentation grenades were exploding like a string of firecrackers. In spite of this, Cpl. Keister managed to pull the wounded Marine to a ditch, put a tourniquet on the wounded leg and covered his head with sand bags to protect him.

To assist L.Cpl. Derenick, Cpl Keister had to leave his rifle behind. Now he went back for it. As Keister describes:

The only way to do this was just like John Wayne would have. Fortunately, there was a fire on this side of the hill, so I was able to see where I was going. I started off at a dead run and dove for my rifle. I picked it up and started to shoot at any number of enemy soldiers who were only a few meters in front of "me. They were in the process of attacking the other radio bunker where Sergeant Poppa, and PFC Whitlock were.

One of the Viet Cong went down and the rest backed off just as I finished this magazine. I jumped into the bunker, removed the empty magazine from my rifle, and asked how they were doing. I only heard a few groans. Just then, I heard a thump and I saw a cigarette like glow, which by now I recognized as the lit fuse on a satchel charge, right inside this very little bunker. I heard automatic fire raking the top edge of the bunker. There was no way out and I had about two seconds to figure out my next move. I jumped to one side of the bunker and lay down as flat as I could get, which wasn't very flat."

Cpl Keister survived the satchel charge; but his eardrums were damaged. He describes what happened next:

"I looked out over the edge of the sand bags, where the bunker wall used to be, and saw an enemy soldier coming my way. This guy is what they call a sapper. A sapper's technique is to move very quietly and very slowly, so you do not see them in the confusion of battle while they work their way close enough to plant their charges. I aimed my weapon, pulled the trigger and nothing happened. I tried to put another round in the chamber and again nothing. I don't remember how many times I repeated this action before I decided the explosion had damaged my weapon. The Viet Cong was still coming. Thank God he was moving in slow motion. In a state of panic, and as a last desperate measure, I started to go through the procedure for clearing your weapon, which we had been made to memorize in boot camp. One of the first steps in this procedure is to check your magazine to see if it is properly seated. It was then I finally figured out the damned thing didn't even have a magazine in it and remembered that was why I came in this bunker in the first place. It was now obvious to me that it was my brain that had been damaged by the explosion, not my rifle. I put a new magazine in my rifle, chambered a round, pointed it at the oncoming VC, fired about a four round burst at the sapper, and missed him completely. He was like ten feet in front of me and I missed him. I couldn't believe it. He couldn't believe it. I fired again and he did a back flip with a half gainer and I assumed he was dead.

I then decided to head back to the last two bunkers that had not been blown up yet. I had just gotten out of what was left of the bunker I was in when another satchel charge, maybe the back blast of an RPG (rocket propelled grenade), blew me back towards my original bunker, in the exact opposite direction of where I wanted to go. I tried again, and again another satchel charge blew me off to the side. I tried one more time and yet another satchel charge blew me right where I wanted to go. I arrived at my next bunker with all of the grace of a sack of grain thrown off of a moving truck."

Being convinced the enemy had the bunkers targeted, Corporal Keister tried to convince the Marines in this bunker to abandon it. As he did so, another satchel charge blew up the bunker. Keister was temporarily blinded. As he describes:

"The explosion was like having a huge flash bulb go off right in front of your face. Only, this flash bulb weighed about 10 pounds and was made of plastic explosives. At the moment, I thought it had blown my eyeballs clean out of my head.

Now I was really upset. I was blind and in the middle of the worst fight of my life. Even if I did somehow live through this thing, I didn't think I would ever be able to see again. I was already on the deck, so I started to feel around to find my rifle. I found it and only then did I think of what the hell I planned to do with it.

Then there was some good news. I saw this faint flashing blue light. It was off about ten meters in front of me. I could see! I could see! What was this light anyway? Bad news, it was an enemy machine gun shooting right at me. I felt bits of sand burning into my face from the bullets impacting into the sand bags around my head. I figured this was a good time to duck. I did so and the enemy machine gunner put one bullet across the back of my head and another down my back."

Keister heard another Marine say: "They got Keister, now what will we do?"

These words prompted Corporal Keister to assess how many men he had left who could fight. He called for them to count off. When the count ended at four, including Cpl. Keister, he faced a tough decision. With only 4 of the original 16 men left capable of fighting, the slopes behind him were clear. He could retreat. Yet he didn't want to be the first Recon Marine to retreat from an observation post. His reputation was on the line and he worried of a possible court martial. Nevertheless, he chose the option that posed the best chance for the men he led to survive.

Cpl. Keister ordered the three other men who had answered his roll call to each grab one of the wounded Marines and haul them down the side of the hill. He told them to hide until help arrived. Cpl. Keister took L.Cpl. Derenick, dragging Derenick down the slope. But Derenick got caught in the perimeter wire. Cpl. Keister, worried that trying to force the wounded Marine through the wire would kill him, paused to think of an alternate solution.

At this time artillery rounds from a Marine battery started to impact around him. These were H & I (harassment and interdiction rounds. It was a common practice for the occupants of an observation post to provide a supporting artillery battery with coordinates just outside the perimeter of the observation post where artillery rounds might discourage any penetration of the observation post defenses by the enemy. As Cpl. Keister explains:

"Whenever they (artillery battery) got the urge, they would crank off a few rounds just in case there were any Viet Cong sneaking around outside our perimeter. Of course now it was us who were outside the perimeter. Fortunately the artillery ceased after a few rounds and nobody was hurt."

Cpl. Keister's thoughts now turned to the wounded Marines who might still be on top of the hill. He wanted to rescue them; but knew rushing back up the hill might just be a suicide mission. By now, support aircraft had arrived; but the pilots would need to know the situation on the ground. They needed to know where the Marines were as well as the location of the enemy. Cpl Keister decided to try to make radio contact. As he describes:

"In the bunker, where the satchel charge knocked me out, was the second radio. If I could get to the radio, I could get a hold of battalion and be able to direct the fire of the aircraft overhead. They had this old CH-47 with miniguns that could shoot up the side of the hill where the Viet Cong support element was waiting. This should give the enemy something else to do other than killing the wounded Marines left back on the hill. The radio was the best hope for all of us and that was my prime objective.

I went back up the hill and snuck around behind the other radio bunker and checked it out. Both of those guys were way beyond saving and the radio was shot full of holes. So much for my big plan. Then I saw something that changed everything. The enemy was evacuating their own dead and wounded over the wire in front of my old bunker. They were all bunched up holding the wire down. That was their mistake. I could see them quite clearly by the light of the diesel oil fire that was still burning. I emptied the magazine I had in my rifle and they started to return fire.

While the remaining NVA were retreating, I worked my way to the center of the hill where I thought I would be able to do the most good. It was there I ran into L.Cpl. Gray. He was the squad's M-60 man. His machine gun had jammed after only a few rounds in the initial moments of the attack. A satchel charge had knocked him unconscious and he did not hear my order to retreat. When he came to, he was all by himself. All he could do was lay there and hide amongst the sand bags and watch as almost the entire enemy force bunched together as they moved out their dead and wounded only a few feet from him and his jammed machine gun. L.Cpl. Gray and I stayed in the center of the hill until dawn started to break."

When it was light enough to see, Cpl' Keister went back up the hill. He first found Corpsman Ploetz, who had been severely wounded from the satchel charge and appeared to be coming out of shock. Cpl. Keister assessed he couldn't do much to assist the Corpsman and Ploetz was in no shape to help with the other wounded. Cpl. Keister then found two more Marines whom he thought had been killed when their bunker blew up. They had just regained consciousness, and appeared to be all right except that they'd lost their hearing.

Next, Cpl. Keister located the two radios. One of them just had the handset and the antenna cut off. The other one was shot up pretty bad, but it had a good handset and antenna. He used the good parts of each to make one that worked. Then he called battalion headquarters and learned helicopters had been dispatched to assist them.

He continued to inspect the remains of the observation post. He found Sgt. Hicks, the Company Supply Sergeant who had volunteered for the OP to improve his suntan. Although the Sergeant appeared to be unscathed by the battle at first, when Keister felt for a pulse he discovered the Sergeant was dead. Next he came upon the body of PFC Smith who apparently had burned to death after a satchel charge ignited a five-gallon can of diesel fuel. Sgt. Poppa,

L.Cpl. Jones, and PFC Whitlock were also dead.

The helicopters arrived to extract the beleaguered Marines. With them came a "reaction force" of other Marines from the Battalion to fight off any enemy forces, who might to continue the assault on the outpost. The wounded were taken to a hospital at China Beach. Cpl. Keister had been hit twice by rifle fire and four times by shrapnel from grenades, some of which the doctors couldn't remove. His eardrums had been ruptured and most of his body burned and scraped by explosives. Still, he, L.Cpl. Luera, and L.Cpl. Gray returned for duty with 1st Recon Battalion. The other wounded were sent home and discharged from the Marine Corps.

Cpl. Keister describes what occurred in the aftermath of his experience on Hill 200 as follows:

"Later reports said a mass grave was found in the general area with 15 or so enemy in it. Only three of our weapons had been fired that night so these enemy soldiers had to have been killed by LCpl. Jones, L.Cpl. Derenick, and myself. Another report came in that a hill similar to 200 was found with a complete mock-up of our positions and wire. Hill 200 was not the high ground in that area, but was the only place from which we could see the whole valley below. Only a few hundred meters from us, the enemy held the high ground and could observe us and make detailed maps of every inch of Hill 200.

First Reconnaissance Battalion immediately rebuilt the hill and refortified it correctly. Good bunkers, good trenches, good wire and lots of it. They left a reinforced platoon of 25 men, with an experienced patrol leader, to hold it. Three weeks later, the VC hit them again. They killed the patrol leader and shot the hill up pretty bad. It took the air wing the whole night to beat the enemy back."

Corporal Roger Keister went on to complete 25 more

long range reconnaissance patrols before leaving Vietnam in November of 1969. He was awarded the Silver Star Medal for his actions on Hill 200. Corpsman Ploetz, returned to the United States for medical treatment. He eventually got naturalized as a citizen.

EPLILOGUE

The stories in the proceeding chapters are only a fraction of those that could be told. The Third Reconnaissance Battalion served in Vietnam from May 1965 to November 1969. The First Reconnaissance Battalion was there from March 1966 to March 1971. A standard tour of duty for a Recon Marine was 12 months; but for many this was cut short by death or disabling injury. This means a lot Marines served and among these men, many others performed heroic actions not told in this book. Since approximately 35 years have passed since the war ended for the Recon Marines, it is difficult to reconstruct what happened.

The best information, of course, comes from the Recon Marines who served, their family members and friends. In the past 35 years many who survived the war and their buddies have since died. Family members and friends are hard to locate as many men have a "Home of Record" listed as a major metropolitan area. Even when the Marines, family members and friends can be located, they have trouble remembering significant facts.

I challenge the reader to try to find out if there are any Recon Marines who served in Vietnam in your local community. The internet provides a good starting place. Both the 1st and 3rd Marine Reconnaissance Battalions have associations that maintain websites that list names of members of the associations as well as the known who are now dead. Again, they don't have information on all who served; but there may be someone listed from your town or a nearby one.

Local Veteran's groups may provide additional information. Perhaps former Recon Marines are members of these groups. The local library may also have archives of hometown newspapers containing stories of local heroes. There are also several books written by Marines who served as Reconnaissance Marines. If you can't find any such books in your library, you can search online bookstores for titles. Then give the title to the local librarian or your school librarian and ask them to order it for the library.

Good hunting!

GLOSSARY

A-6: The A-6 was a carrier-based attack jet aircraft named the *Intruder*. It carried a crew of 2 and could be armed with rockets, bombs or napalm.

Actual: This was a term used to refer to the commander of a unit. Often it was used in radio communications to avoid divulging the actual name, rank or unit designations over the airwaves, making radio transmissions more secure from the enemy. It was usually used with a code name. For example, *Stone Pit* Actual, would be the commander of the unit with the code name, *Stone Pit*.

AK-47: A standard rifle used by the North Vietnamese Army and Viet Cong. It could be fired as an automatic or semi-automatic.

Amtrak: An armored vehicle used for transporting troops and supplies. Specially designed to bring Marines onshore from ships, it was capable of traveling on land or sea.

AO (Air Observer): The term refers to the pilot of a propeller-driven, fixed-wing aircraft. Several types of aircraft were used for the purpose. The aircraft were what people commonly call small planes. They were slower and more maneuverable than jet fighters, thus making it easier to observe activity of either friendly or enemy troops on the ground. They were equipped with machine guns, which the pilot used to support troops on the ground.

Arc Light: The term refers to the mission performed by Air Force B-52 bombers. Flown from remote bases like Kadena AFB in Okinawa, the B-52 could deliver a massive number of bombs on known enemy positions. Marines often referred to such a single strike as "arc-lighting" an area.

Army Special Forces (Green Berets): An elite unit of the U.S. Army, specially trained for operations deep in enemy territory. They carried out operations similar to recon Marines and whether they were more skilled is a subject of debate among recon Marines.

ARVN (Army of Republic of Vietnam): The South Vietnamese Army whom the United States was supporting in the fight against the communists forces.

B-52: A long-range, inter-continental bomber, originally developed by the U.S. Air Force to counter the threat posed by Soviet forces. It was capable of delivering nuclear bombs, but, in Vietnam, was used to deliver a large number of conventional bombs on selected targets. As the bombs were dropped from a high altitude, the enemy wasn't normally aware of the bomber until the bombs began to explode.

Bangalore Torpedo: A device consisting of an explosive charge attached to a long, extendable tube. The Bangalore torpedo was useful in clearing obstacles such as defense perimeter barbed wire from a distance, thus reducing exposure to gunfire from the defenders.

Basic School: The school Marine Officers attended after being commissioned as officers. In this school the officers learned how to lead Marines in infantry and amphibious assault operations.

Body Bag: A bag designed to carry the corpse of those killed in action from the site of the casualty to a place where the body could be prepared for burial.

Booby Trap: Devices used to kill or injure that were hidden and usually activated (sprung) by pressure when stepped on or by tripping on a wire. Some used explosives; but there were a great variety of devices see **Punji sticks** for an additional example.

Bunker: Usually built partially above and partially below ground, bunkers served to protect men, ammunition, and supplies from the enemy assaulting with rifles, grenades, and mortars. Most were not strong enough to withstand direct hits from mortar or artillery rounds or concentrated explosives.

C-4: A plastic explosive that could be molded by hand like clay.

CH-46: The CH-46 Sea Knight was a medium-lift helicopter. It had twin rotors and transported both men and supplies. Troops entered from a ramp lowered in the rear. It was equipped with two machine guns on each side of the aircraft near the front. The combat crew consisted of a pilot, copilot, crew chief, and two aerial gunners.

Chi-Com: This was a slang abbreviation for Chinese Communist, usually used as an adjective to refer the origin of manufacture of weapons, grenades, etc. used by the Viet Cong and NVA.

CIDG (Civilian Irregular Defense Group): Ethnic minorities trained by the U.S. Special Forces for village defense and operations similar to those of the Green Berets and recon Marines.

Cobra: A helicopter specially designed for attacking enemy positions. Manned by a crew of two, it carried a minigun that fired 7.62-mm bullets at a rapid rate of fire and a 40-mm grenade launcher in a nose turret. It also had machine guns and 2.75-in rocket pods mounted on stub wings.

C-Rations: Specially prepared meals eaten by troops in the field where it was not possible to have hot meals. The C-rations consisted of cans of food with a plastic bag of accessories (plastic spoons, toilet paper, etc.). All the items in a single C-ration were packed in a compact box. A typical meal consisted of a can containing a main course (i.e. beans and weenies), a can of fruit, and a desert (i.e. pound cake) in a can.

CS Gas: This was a "tear" gas used to coax the enemy out of bunkers and caves. Special grenades carried the gas. Although most effective in confined spaces, even in the open, the gas would cause coughing and vomiting. The Marines carried gas masks to prevent being affected by the gas.

Demilitarized Zone (DMZ): The DMZ was a narrow strip of land that divided North from South Vietnam. The zone was often occupied by Communist forces and thus was hardly demilitarized.

F-4 Phantom: The F-4 was the primary jet aircraft used to support Marine ground troops. Although it could be flown from an aircraft carrier, Phantom squadrons were also located at land bases in South Vietnam. It could deliver, bombs, missiles, and napalm on enemy positions.

Fire Mission: This term refers to an artillery or mortar strike. Troops in the field would provide map coordinates to a remote base when requesting a fire mission. As the rounds were fired, the troops would provide additional information to the remote base to make necessary corrections to hit the targeted areas.

Fire Support Base: A base that provided artillery support.

Gook: A slang term used to describe both VC and NVA.

Grenades: Compact explosive devices either thrown by hand or fired from special guns. There were a variety of types of grenades. The fragmentation grenade was designed to explode at a timed interval and propel bits of metal (shrapnel) to kill or wound. The incendiary was designed to burn or melt through metal. The smoke grenade was used as a signaling device or to screen troops from enemy detection. Illumination grenades were used to light up the area where it impacted.

Grunt: A slang term for infantryman.

H & I Rounds: Artillery batteries fired H & I (harassment and interdiction) rounds into where they suspected the enemy was located without specific targets. The rounds were usually fired at random with regard to time and place. The purpose was to discourage enemy infiltration into those areas.

Hanoi: The Capitol of North Vietnam.

Harbor Site: The place where a recon team beds down for the night.

High-speed Trail: This was a trail that was usually well worn with little vegetation on the ground caused by frequent travel of enemy troops. High-speed meant that one could travel the trail on foot rapidly without having to push through brush. The VC and NVA transported much of their supplies along trails rather than roads since trails were often not visible due to the canopy provided by trees on either side of the trail.

HLZ (Helicopter Landing Zone): A HLZ was a place with sufficient area for a helicopter to land.

Hootch: This was a slang term referring to a place of residence. The Vietnamese "hootches" might be thatched roof huts. Those occupied by the Marines likely had corrugated metal roofs on top of a wooden framed structure with screened sections for windows.

Illumination Round: Special artillery rounds that would light up an area at night.

Insert officer: The insert officer was an officer from a Marine reconnaissance unit who flew aboard the helicopter containing a recon team. He didn't go in with the team; but coordinated the insert of the team with the aircraft crew.

Jungle Penetrator: This was a device consisting of a bar attached to a cable. The bar served as a seat. Using this device, it was possible to hoist a single man from the jungle to a helicopter. As the jungle penetrator was a simple device, it could easily be lowered through dense jungle.

LAAW (Light Antitank Assault Weapon): The LAAW was a weapon designed for an infantryman to use against tanks. Its primary advantage was that it was light and thus easy to carry. It was a single use weapon. Once the LAAW was fired, it couldn't be reused. It was often used against targets other than tanks.

Liberty: Liberty is a term to describe sailors or Marines getting the opportunity to enjoy a night off from their duties away from their duty station.

LZ (same as HLZ)

M-79: The M-79 was grenade launcher. A hand-held weapon, it had the appearance of a sawed-off shot gun. It fired 40-mm grenades. The slang name for the M-79 was "the blooper". Blooper referred to the sound made by the M-79 when a round was fired.

Medevac (Medical Evacuation): The term Medevac normally referred to the emergency removal of a sick, wounded or injured man from the field, usually by helicopter.

Mortar: The mortar is a smooth-bore, muzzle-loaded, high-angle-of-fire weapon. It consists of a metal tub (barrel), a base plug and a fixed firing pin for drop firing. To fire the mortar a round is dropped down the tube. When the round reaches the base plate of the mortar tube, the firing pin ignites the round. The pressure of the gas produced by the burning propelling charge drives the round up and out of the barrel. The round has stabilizing fins that provide a smooth trajectory. There are different types of mortar rounds designed for various purposes, one of which is to deliver an explosive on an enemy position.

Napalm: Napalm is an incendiary mixture of benzene, gasoline and polystyrene. Aircraft dropped napalm on enemy positions to burn away any covering brush.

National Liberation Front: The National Liberation Front was the political wing of the Viet Cong. Cong is short for Cong-san, which means Communist. The military wing was called the People's Liberation Armed Forces.

OP (Observation Post): The military set up observation posts at key points to observe enemy movements. These were generally located on the top of hills that offered the best view of an area of suspected enemy movement. Many were equipped with special scope called an integrated observation device (IOD) which allowed the observer to spot enemy movement around the clock and from which the observer could determine direction and range to a target. Reconnaissance Marines were assigned responsibility for defending several of these. Normally a platoon of recon Marines would spend about two weeks on an observation post before being replaced by another platoon. Guarding an OP was usually a rest assignment for the recon troops as their main duty was to stand guard. OP defenses generally consisted of barbed and/or concertina wire placed around the perimeter, trip flares, claymore mines, and crew served weapons like a mortar or 50-caliber machine gun. Walls of sandbags and bunkers provided protection for the Marines.

OV-10: The OV-10 was a propeller driven, fixed wing aircraft, commonly called the *Bronco*. It was equipped with two 7.62-mm Gatling guns and could also carry up to 3,600 pounds of other ordinance such as bombs and rockets. Air Observers flew this plane in support of troops on the ground.

PRC-25: The PRC-25 was the radio carried by a recon team in the field. It was worn as a backpack.

Punji Sticks: Punji Stick or Punji Stake is a type of a non-explosive booby trap. Usually it was several pointed and sharpened bamboo sticks mounted vertically in a pit in the ground, covered with grass, brush or similar material to camouflage its location. The tip of the punji stick was frequently smeared with feces, urine or other contaminants to promote infection in the wound created by the sharpened stick penetrating the soldier's skin. The point of penetration was usually in the foot or lower leg area. Pungi sticks were not necessarily meant to kill the person who stepped on it; rather it was designed as a non-lethal weapon to wound the enemy and tie up their unit while the victim was evacuated to a medical facility.

R & R: R&R stands for rest and relaxation. During a normal 12-month tour a Marine was allowed to take a week off for a vacation. He would be flown to one of several sites such as Bangkok, Thailand, Sydney, Australia, or Hong Kong, China. There were also opportunities for in-country (within South Vietnam) R&R. China Beach near Danang was one location where a unit like a recon team might be allowed to take a few days off for R&R.

Radio Relay: A radio relay was a location where radio messages could be received and retransmitted to their destination. Radio waves travel along "line of sight" and can be blocked by mountainous terrain. To solve this problem, radio relays were established at high points to relay the transmissions from a team in a valley for instance to operational headquarters.

Reaction Force: The reaction force was a group of Marines, either from the reconnaissance battalion or an infantry unit that was prepared to assist a team in contact with the enemy in the bush. The reaction force usually consisted of a platoon and could be quickly air-lifted by helicopter to the trouble spot.

RPG (Rocket Propelled Grenade): The RPG is a rocket that can be fired from the shoulder like a rifle. The rocket is designed to be an anti-tank weapon, but the NVA and VC used the weapon in Vietnam much like a grenade launcher.

Sapper: These were units of the Communists forces specially trained to penetrate the Marine defenses and inflict maximum casualties. They were adept in making their way through the barbed and concertina wire defensive perimeters, conducting swift and punishing attacks, then withdraw. Their objective was to inflict maximum casualties, destroy equipment, ordinance and installations, not to seize and hold territory.

Satchel Charge: A satchel charge is a cloth or plastic bag containing explosive equipped with a fuse to allow a delay before igniting the explosive. The fuse is ignited and the bag thrown at the target (i.e. a bunker) where it explodes.

Shackle Sheets: Sheets of paper containing code for coding radio messaged.

Starlight Scope: A specially developed telescope that allows the user to see at night.

Tail End Charlie: The last man on a recon patrol. His responsibility was to see no one snuck up on the team from behind.

UH-1 Huey: The UH-1 helicopter was the most widely used helicopter in Vietnam. Dubbed the "Huey" because the original designation was HU-1A, this helicopter transported troops, was used for Medevacs and as a gunship. It had a crew of two and could carry as many as 12 troops. Hueys could be armed with M-60 machine guns, 20-mm cannon, 2.75-inch rockets, and a 40-mm grenade launcher. Troops boarded the helicopter from the sides.

UH-34: The UH-34 helicopter was another helicopter used to transport troops and evacuate wounded in Vietnam. The UH-34 was gradually replaced by the CH-46 because the CH-46 could carry heavier loads, was faster, and was easier for the troops to board or disembark.

United Service Organization (USO): The USO is a nonprofit, congressionally chartered, private organization that relies on the generosity of individuals, organizations and corporations to support USO activities. The USO is not part of the U.S. Government but is supported by the President of the United States and the Department of Defense. Each President has been the Honorary Chairman of the USO since its inception. The USO mission is to provide morale, welfare and recreation-type services to our men and women in uniform. One activity they sponsored in Vietnam was the USO show. A typical show consisted of a group of entertainers, usually musicians that traveled among the bases and performed for the troops. The most famous of these was the Bob Hope show, which usually performed during the Christmas season. However, many of the troops could enjoy more frequent visits by groups from the Philippines or Australia.

Viet Cong: The Viet Cong were the Communist forces of South Vietnam who sought to take control of the government. (See National Liberation Front above.)